CATALOGUE

OF

LIBRARY,

BELONGING TO THE

NATIONAL HOME FOR DISABLED VOLUNTEER SOLDIERS,

(NORTHWESTERN BRANCH)

Near MILWAUKEE, Wisconsin.

National Soldiers' Home Printing Office.
NEAR MILWAUKEE, WISCONSIN.

1875.

HISTORICAL SKETCH.

A well selected and miscellaneous collection of books and other literature suited to the general reader, has ever been considered by the management of the Home to be an almost indispensable requisite to proper government and control; and therefore early in the history of the Institution, efforts were made to secure voluntary contributions from interested persons, and more recently an annual expenditure has been made from the contingent fund to further the project, which has at length assumed the character and proportions of a *Library*. It is apparent, from the inscriptions upon many of the volumes which have evidently been longest in use, that the effort to obtain voluntary contributions was, in some degree, responded to by benevolent sympathizers. On the fly-leaves of several books is written: "Eight Wisconsin Battery Library Association;" on a few, "Presented by citizens of Columbus, Wis.;" on others, "Presented by First Unitarian Church Society, Boston, through Rev. Mr. GANNET;" and some two or three hundred volumes contain a slip on which is printed: "*The L. B. Schwabe Library*, named by the Honorable Board of Managers, July 2, 1869—Major-Gen. B. F. Butler, President; Hon. Lewis B. Gunckel, Secretary." A few months later, as appears from the minutes of the Board, its action naming the Library was rescinded.

Additions have been made, from time to time, as the funds devoted to this object would allow; a large and valuable collection of Executive and Congressional Documents have been obtained from Washington through Hon. Alexander Mitchell, and other members of Congress; and complete sets, so far as possible, of Reports of the Adjutant-Generals of the several loyal States, issued during the Rebellion, have recently been obtained. During the past year, nearly eleven hundred dollars were expended for books by the Commandant of the Home, General EDWARD W. HINCKS, adding many valuable standard and popular works. The Library was then classified and a new catalogue made.

The new books were purchased of Harper Brothers, and D. Appleton & Company, New York; and the gentlemen last named have manifested their interest in the Library by donating to it the new edition of the American Cyclopedia.

GEO. W. BARBER,
Chaplain and Librarian.

NATIONAL HOME, NEAR MILWAUKEE, WIS.,
JULY, 1875.

LIBRARY RULES.

1.—The Library will be open daily from eight o'clock A. M., until nine P. M. Hours for obtaining books, eight to eleven A. M., and seven to eight P. M. (Sundays excepted).

2.—Encyclopedias and Books of Reference marked in the Catalogue with an asterisk (*), will not be taken from the Rooms, but may be consulted in the Library.

3.—One Book only will be taken at a time, and retained for a period not exceeding two weeks.

4.—Persons availing themselves of the privileges of the Library will be held responsible, not only for the return of books to the Library, but for all soiling, marking, or other injury of the books while in their care.

5.—Before granting a Furlough or Discharge, the Commandant must be assured, by certificate from the Librarian, or otherwise, that the applicant has returned all books taken by him from the Library.

6.—When through reading a Paper, place the file in proper order upon the rack, with the heading of the paper outward.

7.—No person will be permitted to cut, mark, tear, or otherwise injure books, papers, magazines, or other property pertaining to the Library, nor to remove from the Rooms any article belonging thereto, except by proper authority.

8.—Decorum will be observed in the Library Rooms in respect to dress, removing hats, etc. Loud reading, conversation, and all unnecessary noise, is forbidden.

9.—Willful disregard of these Rules will be debar the offender from the privileges of the Library Rooms, and render him liable to such other penalty as the Commandant may direct.

ARRANGEMENT OF CATALOGUE.

Subjoined to the Catalogue proper will be found:

In the Catalogue proper:

For POETICAL WORKS see *Poems, Poetry, etc.*

HISTORICAL WORKS are arranged under the head of *History* and *Historical.*

When there are several works by the same author, they will be found under the authors surname in its alphabetical order.

---

* Harper's Select Novels will also be found under their respective titles in the Catalogue proper

CATALOGUE.

NO.	TITLE.	AUTHOR.
958.	A Diary,	Frederika Bremer.
1056.	A Girl's Romance, and other Tales,	Frederick W. Robinson.
1054.	A Golden Sorrow,	Mrs. Cashel Hoey.
1054.	A Good Investment,	William Flagg.
1049.	A Life's Assizes,	Mrs. J. H. Riddell.
1217.	A Miller's Story of the War,	Erckmann-Chatrain.
1062.	A Princess of Thule,	William Black.
1061.	A Simpleton,	Charles Reade.
1046.	A Siren,	T. Adolphus Trollope.
1008.	A Strange Story,	Edward Lytton Bulwer.
980.	A Whim,	G. P. R. James.
1009.	Abel Drake's Wife,	John Saunders.
1854.	Abernethy, John, Memoirs of,	George Macilwain.
1583.	Abominations of Modern Society,	De Witt Talmage.
1603.	Abolition of Slave Trade,	(Evidence before House of Com.)
1398.	Adam Bede,	George Eliot.
956.	Adam Brown,	H. Smith.
529.	Adams, John Quincy, Life of,	Josiah Quincy.
1503–5.	Addison's Works, 3 Vols.,	Joseph Addison.
988.	Adelaide Lindsay,	Mrs. Marsh.
1157.	Adele (Tale),	Julia Kavanah.
1334.	Adventures of Philip,	William M. Thackeray.
1519.	Adventures of Ruben Davidger,	James Greenwood.
1520.	ditto ditto	ditto.
1758.	Adventures beyond the Mississippi,	Albert D. Richardson.
2158.	Advice to a Young Preacher,	Joseph Parker.
14.	Æschylus' Tragedies,	Theodore A. Buckley.
1408.	Afloat and Ashore,	J. Fennimore Cooper.
584.	Africa, Interior of,	H. M. Stanley.
247.	Africa, Discovery and Adventures in,	Murray-Jameson-Wilson.
997.	Agatha's Husband,	Miss Mulock

NO.	TITLE.	AUTHOR.
2135.	Age of the World and Signs of the Times,	R. C. Shimeall.
2256.	Aids to Devotion.	Bickersteth-Watts-Henry.
963.	Agincourt,	G. P. R. James.
1021.	Agnes,	Mrs. Oliphant.
997.	Agnes Scrrell,	G. P. R. James.
294.	Agriculture,	John Armstrong.
302.	Agriculture and Chemistry,	Le Compte Chaptal.
1590.	Agricultural Chemistry,	Johnston.
991.	Aims and Obstacles,	G. P. R. James.
665.	Alabama and Sumpter,	Raphael Semms.
978.	Alamance.	
872.	Alarm to Unconverted Sinners,	Joseph Alleine.
1054.	Albert Lunel,	Lord Brougham.
1031.	Alec Forbes,	George MacDonald.
286.	Alexander the Great,	J. Williams.
1212.	Alfred Hagart's Household,	Alexander Smith.
631.	Alfred the Great,	Thomas Hughes.
1655.	Alhambra,	Washington Irving.
955.	Alice,	Edward Lytton Bulwer.
1475.	ditto	ditto.
1025.	All in the Dark,	J. Sheridan Le Fanu.
1624.	Alroy,	B. Disraeli.
2145.	Altar at Home, Prayers, etc.,	Unitarian Clergymen of Boston.
968.	Amaury,	Alexander Dumas.
192–3.	American Adventure, 2 Vols.,	(Harpers' Select Library.)
1298.	American Baron,	James De Mille.
506–7.	American Conflict, 2 Vols.,	Horace Greeley.
1064–79.	*American Cyclopedia, 16 Vols.,	Ripley-Dana.
1080.	*American Cyclopedia, (Annual), 7 Vols.,	1861. ditto.
1081.	ditto ditto	1862. ditto.
1082.	ditto ditto	1863. ditto.
1083.	ditto ditto	1864. ditto.
1084.	ditto ditto	1865. ditto.
1085.	ditto ditto	1866. ditto.
1886.	ditto ditto	1867. ditto.
1087.	ditto ditto	1868. ditto.
1088–1103.	*American Cyclopedia, (revised edition,) 16 Vols.,	Ripley-Dana.

NO.	TITLE.	AUTHOR.
443.	American Family in Germany,	J. Ross Browne.
172–3.	American Husbandry, 2 Vols.,	Gaylord-Tucker.
546.	American Institute, Transactions of, 1857, Secretary's Report.	
1594.	American Miscellany,	Francis C. Woodworth.
1924.	ditto	ditto.
695.	American Monthly Magazine, Vols. 34–35, 1843,	Graham's.
696.	ditto ditto Vol. 43, 1853,	Graham's.
1516.	American Oratory, Compiled by Member of Philadelphia Bar.	
738.	American Review, A Whig Journal, 1845.	
739.	ditto ditto 1846.	
740.	ditto ditto 1846.	
741.	ditto ditto 1847.	
742.	ditto ditto 1848.	
743.	ditto ditto 1848.	
744.	ditto ditto 1849.	
244.	American Revolution, Tales of,	(Harpers' Select Library.)
847.	American's Guide, Constitution of U. S. and several States.	
342.	Amoor Regions, Travels in the,	T. W. Atkinson.
961.	Amy Herbert,	Miss Sewell.
1879.	Anatomy, Physiology, etc.,	T. S. Lambert.
1873.	Ancient America,	John D. Baldwin.
1778.	Andes and the Amazon,	James Orton.
1272.	Andreas Hofer,	Louisa Muhlback.
2246.	Anecdotes of the Ministry,	Daniel Smith.
1832.	Animal Locomotion,	J. B. Pettigrew.
207.	Animal Mechanism,	John H. Griscomb.
995.	Anna Hammer,	M. Temme.
1050.	Anne Furness.	
1630.	Anne of Geierstein,	Walter Scott.
1014.	Annis Warleigh's Fortune,	Holme Lee.
1296.	An Open Question,	James De Mille.
1049.	Anteros,	George H. Lawrence.
1631.	Antiquary, The,	Walter Scott.
1241.	Antonia,	George Sand.
442.	Apachee Country,	J. Ross Browne.
959.	Arabella Stuart,	G. P. R. James.
634.	Arabian Nights Entertainment.	
650.	Arctic Adventure in search of Franklin,	Epes Sargent.

No.	TITLE.	AUTHOR.
61.	Arctic Regions, Discovery in	Sir John Barrow.
371.	Arctic Researches,	Charles F. Hall.
375.	Argument at Geneva.	Cushing-Evarts-Waite.
418.	Army Life on the Border,	R. B. Marcy.
344.	Army of the Potomac,	William Swinton.
636.	Army of the Potomac,	A. S. Castleman.
678.	*Army and Navy Journal, Vol. 1, 1863–64.	
679.	ditto do 2, 1864–65.	
680.	ditto do 3, 1865–66.	
681.	ditto do 4, 1866–67.	
682.	ditto do 5, 1867–68.	
683.	ditto do 6, 1868–69,	
684.	ditto do 7, 1869-70,	
31.	Arnold, Benedict, Life and Treason,	Jared Sparks.
962.	Arrah Neil; or, Times of Old,	G. P. R. James.
963.	Arthur Arundel,	H. Smith.
991.	Arthur Conway,	E. H. Milman.
848.	Artillery Instructions—1826,	Board of Officers, U. S. A.
969.	Ascanio,	Alexander Dumas.
1607.	Asphodel.	
1656.	Astoria,	Washington Irving.
80.	Astronomer, The Practical,	Thomas Dick.
1919.	Astronomy,	John Brocklesby.
203.	Astronomy,	Thomas Dick.
2078.	Astronomy of the Bible,	O. M. Mitchell.
1604.	Astronomy and Geography,	Emma Willard.
1005.	Athelings, The,	Margaret Oliphant.
657.	Athens, Its Rise and Fall,	Edward Lytton Bulwer.
714.	Atlantic Monthly, Vol. 27, 1871.	
715.	ditto Vol. 28, 1871.	
1193.	At Last,	Marion Harland.
1134.	At Odds,	Baroness Tautphoeus.
1704.	At the Back of the North Wind,	George MacDonald.
999.	Aubrey,	Mrs. Marsh.
1567.	Aunt Jane's Hero,	E. Prentiss.
1722.	Aunt Jo's Scrap Bag,	Louisa M. Alcott.
1010.	Aurora Floyd,	Miss E. Braddon.
968.	Author's Daughter,	Mary Howitt.

NO.	TITLE.	AUTHOR.
1001.	Avillon,	Miss Mulock.
1260.	Awful Disclosures of the Nunnery,	Maria Monk.
1125.	Bachelor of the Albany.	
1155.	Bachelor's Story.	
293.	Bacon's and Lock's Essays,	Francis Bacon, etc.
1042.	Baffled,	Julia Goddard.
958.	Banker's Wife; or, Court and City,	Mrs. Gore.
3217.	Baptism, Mode and Subject,	Milo P. Jewett.
1014.	Barbara's History,	Amelia B. Edwards.
227.	Barbary State.,	Michael Russell.
1046.	Barchester Towers,	Anthony Trollope.
1555.	Barclays, of Boston,	Mrs. H. G. Otis.
1426.	Barnaby Rudge,	Charles Dickens.
1305–6.	ditto 2 Vols.,	ditto.
1815.	Barnum's Struggles and Triumphs,	P. T. Barnum.
1124.	Barriers Burned Away,	Edward P. Roe.
1010.	Barrington,	Charles Lever.
1615.	Battle of the Books,	Gail Hamilton.
1163.	Beatrice (Novel),	Julia Kavanagh.
975.	Beauchamp,	G. P. R. James.
1266.	Beaumarchais,	A. E. Brachvogel.
1152.	Beauty and the Beast,	Bayard Taylor.
1160.	Bede's Charity,	Hesba Stretton.
1132.	Beechcroft.	
1040.	Beggar on Horseback,	James Payn.
1867–8.	Beginning of Life, 2 Vols.,	H. C. Bastian.
2247.	Behold the Lamb of God,	E. N. Kirk.
1245.	Belford Regis, Sketches of a Country Town,	Mary R. Mitford.
1019.	Belial.	
761.	Belinda.	
1021.	Belton Estate,	Anthony Trollope.
1042.	Beneath the Wheels.	
1271,	Berlin and Sans Souci,	Louisa Mehlbach.
1111.	ditto ditto	ditto.
1028.	Bernthal,	ditto.
1253.	Best Fellow in the World,	Mrs. J McN. Wright.
1632.	Betrothed Highland Widow,	Walter Scott.
2052.	Better Covenant,	Francis Goode.

No.	TITLE.	AUTHOR.
786.	Beulah (Novel),	Augusta J. Evans.
1150.	Beverly; or, The White Mask,	M. T. Walworth.
1758.	Beyond the Mississippi,	Albert D. Richardson.
1763.	ditto ditto	ditto.
2137.	Bible and Civil Government,	J. M. Mathews.
2236.	Bible Companion.	
324.	Bible Dictionary,	William Smith.
2018.	Bible Hand-Book,	Joseph Angus.
1991.	Bible History, Illustrated,	William Smith.
2046.	Bible Music,	Francis Jacox.
2066.	Bible Readings for a Year,	John Kitto.
2244.	Bible Scholars' Manuel,	B. K. Pierce.
2129.	Bible Temperance,	Willliam M. Thayer.
2127.	Biblical Antiquities,	John W. Nevin.
81.	Biblical Legends,	G. Weil.
400.	Biographical and Critical Miscellanies,	William H. Prescott.
161–3.	Biography, American—3 Vols.,	Jeremy Belknap.
29–38.	Biography, American—10 Vols.,	Jared Sparks.
641.	Biography, American,	C. A. Goodrich.
1605.	Biographies of Scientific Men, 1st Series,	Francois Arago.
1606.	ditto ditto 2d Series,	ditto
958.	Birthright, The,	Mrs. Gore.
2087.	Bishop Hebers, Life and Writings,	American Clergyman.
604.	Bivouac and Battlefields,	G. F. Noyes.
1455.	Black Diamonds,	J. C. Hannibal.
1029.	Black Sheep,	Edmund Yates.
1463.	Bleak House,	Charles Dickens.
1307–8.	ditto 2 Vols.,	ditto.
498.	Blockade of Phalsburg.	
1915.	Blind Man's Offering,	B. B. Bowen.
1063.	Blue Ribbon.	
1679.	Boat Builder's Family,	Z. A. Mudge.
449.	Boat Life in Egypt,	William C. Prime.
71.	Body and Mind,	George Moore.
2172.	ditto	ditto.
124–5.	Bonaparte, Napoleon—2 Vols.,	J. G. Lockhard.
372.	Bonaparte, Napoleon, Life of,	M. L. DeL. Ardeche.
256.	Bonaparte, Court and Camp of,	

NO.	TITLE.	AUTHOR.
1657.	Bonneville's Adventures,	Washington Irving.
709.	Book-Keeping,	J. C. Colt.
2108.	Book of Revelation, Lectures on,	William B. Hayden.
1335.	Book of Snobs and Sketches,	William M. Thackeray.
1380.	ditto ditto	ditto.
1441.	Border and Bastille.	
592.	Book of Reminiscences,	R. B. Marcy, U. S. A.
180–1.	Border Wars of American Revolution, 2 Vols.,	W. L. Stone.
967.	Bosom Friend,	Mrs Grey.
1891.	Boston, Book—1837,	B. B. Thatcher.
1221.	Both Sides of the Street,	Mary S. Walker.
799.	Botany for Beginners,	Mrs. A. H. L. Phelps.
1025.	Bound to the Wheel,	John Saunders.
1223.	Boy Hunters,	Captain Mayne Reid.
893.	Boy's and Girls' Book,	Cathe·ine D. Bell.
537.	Boys in Blue,	Mrs. A. H. Hoge.
1549.	Bracebridge Hall,	Washington Irving.
1658.	ditto	ditto.
1035.	Brakespeare,	George Lawrence.
1293.	Brand, Captain of the Centipede,	Harry Gringo.
870.	Brainard, David,	President Edwards.
36.	Brainard, David, Life of,	William B. O. Peabody.
2011.	Brainard, Rev. Thomas, Life of,	M. Brainard.
1409.	Brano,	J. Fennimore Cooper.
966.	Breach of Promise.	
478.	Breakfast, Dinner and Tea.	
2204.	Breathings of the Better Life,	Lucy Larcom.
1048.	Bred in the Bone,	James Payn.
1166.	Bressant,	Julian Hawthorne.
1633.	Bride of Lammermoor,	Walter Scott.
1053.	Bridge of Glass, A,	F. W. Robinson.
201–2.	British America—2 Vols.,	Hugh Murray.
1536.	Brockley Moor,	J. W. L.
1189.	Brooks of Briddlemere,	G. J. W. Melville.
495.	Bronte, Charlotte, Life of,	E. C. Gaskell.
1508–9.	Brougham's Speeches—2 Vols.,	Lord Brougham.
1033½.	Brothers' Bet,	Emilie Flygare Carlen.
980.	Brothers and Sisters,	Frederika Bremer.

No.	TITLE.	AUTHOR.
29.	Brown, Charles B., Life of,	William H. Prescott.
620.	Brown, Capt. John, Life of,	James Redpath.
1008.	Brown, Jones and Robinson,	Anthony Trollope.
1609.	Brown, Capt. C. H., Imprisonment and Escape.	
689.	Brown, Jones and Robinson, American Tour of,	By Toby.
690.	ditto ditto Foreign Tour of,	Richard Doyle.
1034.	Brownlows,	Mrs. Oliphant.
210.	Bruce, James, Life of,	Francis B. Head.
1745.	Buchanan's Administration.	
325.	Buffalo Land,	W. E. Webb.
2219.	Bugle Call,	Volunteer Nurse.
2182.	Building on the Rock,	Mrs. J. M. Parker.
771.	Bunyan, Riches of,	
1510–12.	Burke's Works—3 Vols.,	Edmund Burke.
973.	Bush Rangers,	Charles Rowcroft.
2237.	Burn, General Andrew.	
25.	Butler's Analogy,	Robert Emory.
37.	Cabot, Sebastian, Life of,	Charles Hayward.
1804.	Caged Lion,	Charlotte M. Yonge.
554.	California Book for Travels, etc.,	Charles Nordhoff.
645.	California Life Illustrated,	William Taylor.
1761.	California, Oregon, and Sandwich Islands,	Charles Nordhoff.
2223.	Call to the Uncon·erted,	Richard Baxter.
1031.	Called to Account,	Miss Annie Thomas.
1895.	Camp and Field,	S. C. Smith.
1926.	Camp and March,	Henry D. Grafton.
1914.	Camping Out,	C. A. Stephens.
1385.	Cameron Pride,	Mrs. M. J. Holmes.
1190.	Cancelled Will,	Mrs. Eliza A. Dupuy.
1890.	Capital Punishment,	Charles Spear.
602.	Capture, Prison-Pen, and Escape,	Williard W. Glazier.
1033.	Carlyon's Year,	James Payn.
1019.	Carry's Confession.	
2243.	Caroosso, William, Memoirs of,	Autobiography.
1456.	Cast Up by the Sea,	Samuel W. Baker.
621.	Cartwright, Peter,	Autobiography.
1032.	Caste.	
996.	Castle Avon,	Mrs. Marsh.

NO.	TITLE.	AUTHOR.
1648.	Castle Dangerous,	Walter Scott.
759.	Catalogue of Milwaukee Young Men's Library.	
733.	Catalogue Soldiers' Home Library, Augusta, Me.,	G. W. Barber.
734.	Catalogue Soldiers' Home Library, Milwaukee, Wis ,	G. W. Barber.
633.	Cave Life in Vicksburg,	A Lady.
634.	ditto	ditto.
855–6.	Cavalry Tactics—2 Vols.,	P. St. G. Cooke.
857.	Cavalry Tactics (Dismounted), 1841.	
858.	ditto (Mounted), 1841.	
859.	ditto (Evolutions of a Regiment), 1841.	
1476.	Caxtons,	Edward Lytton Bulwer.
982.	ditto	ditto.
1052.	Cecil's Tryst,	James Payn.
2191.	Celestial Dawn,	W. F. Evans.
298.	Celestial Scenery,	Thomas Dick.
530.	Central Asia, Travels in,	Arminius Vambery.
2138.	Centenary of Wesleyan Methodism,	Thomas Jackson.
1172.	Cerise: A Tale of Last Century,	G. J. W. Melville.
1410.	Chain Bearer,	J. Fennimore Cooper.
967.	Chance Medley,	Thomas Colley Grattan.
1452.	Chandos,	Ouida.
2013–15.	Channing's Works—6 Vols. in 3,	William E. Channing.
1872.	Character,	Samuel Smiles.
753.	Charities and Reform. Wisconsin, 1871.	
998.	Charles Auchester,	E. Berger.
512–13.	Charles the Bold—2 Vols.,	John F. Kirk.
386–8.	Charles the Fifth—3 Vols.,	William H. Prescott.
1034.	Charlotte's Inheritance,	M. E. Braddon.
1814.	Chateau Frissac,	Olive Logan.
960.	Chatsworth,	Ward.
1941.	Chemical Instructor,	Amos Eaton.
1921.	Chemistry,	Edward L. Youmans.
239.	Chemistry, Elements of,	James Renwick.
346.	Chesterfield's Works,	Lord Chesterfield.
971.	Chevalier d'Harmental,	Dumas.
557.	Chicago Fire, (1871),	James W. Shehan.
2193.	Children in the Temple,	H. Clay Trumbull.

No.	TITLE.	AUTHOR.
184–5.	China and the Chinese—2 Vols.,	John F. Davis.
1560.	China: Its State and Prospects,	W. H. Medhurst.
586–7.	Chinese Empire, Travels in—2 Vols.,	M. Huc.
475–6.	Chinese' Social Life—2 Vols.,	Justus Doolittle.
133.	Chivalry, History of,	G. P. R. James.
2058.	Christ and His Apostles,	John Fleetwood.
1998.	Christ, Life of,	Henry Ward Beecher.
2144.	Christ, Life of,	Ernest Renan.
2205.	Christian Doctrine of Prayer,	James F. Clarke.
2190.	Christian Hymns.	
2177.	Christian Instructor,	Josiah Hopkins.
1726.	Christian Life in England, in Olden Times.	
2054.	ditto ditto ditto.	
2106.	Christian Perfection,	George Peck.
1997.	Christian Religion True,	Emanuel Swedenborg.
2139.	Christian Retrospect and Register,	Robert Baird.
2168.	Christian Year.	
2023.	Christianity and Its Conflicts,	E. E. Marcy.
2033.	Christianity and Skepticism,	Boston Lectures (1870).
2034.	ditto ditto	ditto (1871).
304.	Christianity, Evidences of,	William Paley.
2178.	ditto ditto	ditto.
1309.	Christmas Books,	Charles Dickens.
1336.	Christmas Books,	William M. Thackeray.
622.	Christmas in the West Indies,	Charles Kingsley.
1464.	Christmas Stories, etc ,	Charles Dickens.
1570–2.	Christus: Divine Tragedy—3 Vols.,	Henry W. Longfellow.
1497.	Chronicles of Carlingford.	
973.	Chronicles of Clovernook,	Douglass Jerrold, *et al.*
697–9.	Church Offerings for all Seasons—Vols. 2, 4, 5.	
2032.	Church Polity of the Pilgrims,	J. W. Wellman.
319.	Cicero's Offices and Moral Works,	Cyrus R. Edmonds.
16.	ditto ditto	ditto.
17.	Cicero's Select Orations,	O. D. Yonge.
975.	Cinq-Mars,	Alfred DeVigny.
1032.	Circe,	Babington White.
279.	Circumnavigation of the Globe,	Harpers' Select Library
970.	Citizen of Prague,	Mary Howitt.

NO.	TITLE.	AUTHOR.
1742.	City of the Saints (Salt Lake),	Richard F. Burton.
373.	Civil Policy of America,	John W. Draper.
326–8.	Civil War in America—3 Vols.,	John W. Draper.
229.	Classical Antiquities,	Joseph Salkeld.
1028.	Claverings,	Anthony Trollope
1005.	Clerical Life,	George Eliot.
1368.	Cloister and Hearth,	Charles Reade.
1126.	Cloud on the Heart,	A. S. Roe.
998.	Clouded Happiness,	Countess D'Orsay.
1662–4.	Columbus, Life and Voyages of, 3 Vols.,	Washington Irving.
2255.	Commerce and Christianity,	Hollis Read.
1878.	Company Clerk, (Military,)	August V. Kautz.
2060.	Complete Duty of Man,	Henry Venn.
972.	Commander of Malta,	Eugene Sue.
2068.	Commentary on Matthew and Mark—Vol. 1,	Albert Barnes.
2069.	ditto Luke and John—Vol. 2,	ditto.
2070.	ditto Matthew and Mark—Vol. 1,	ditto.
2071.	ditto Luke and John—Vol. 2,	ditto.
989.	Commissioner,	G. P. R. James.
1536.	Common-Place Book,	Robert Southey.
735–6.	Common School Journal, (Mass,)—Vols. 2 and 3.	
2129.	Communion Wine, etc.,	William M. Thayer.
538.	Confederate States, and Battle of Bull Run,	J. G. Barnard.
2053.	Congregationalism and Methodism,	Z. K. Hawley.
1625.	Coningsby,	B. Disraeli.
314.	Conquest and Self-Conquest,	Harpers' Select Library.
1659.	Conquest of Granada,	Washington Irving.
391–3.	Conquest of Mexico—3 Vols.,	William H. Prescott.
389–90.	Conquest of Peru—2 Vols.,	ditto.
1829.	Conservation of Energy,	Balfour Stewart.
1002.	Constance Herbert,	Geraldine E. Jewsbury.
984	Constance Lindsay,	C. G. H.
257.	Constitution of Man,	George Combe.
1785.	ditto,	ditto.
318.	Constitution of the U. S.: Exposition of,	Joseph Story.
900.	Constitution of the United States, etc.	
331.	Constitutional History of England,	Henry Hallam.
223.	Constitutional Jurisprudence,	William A. Duer.

No.	TITLE.	AUTHOR.
357–61.	Consulate and Empire—5 Vols.,	M. A. Thiers.
1626.	Contarini Fleming,	B. Disraeli.
2133.	Contemplations and Letters,	Henry Dorney.
2110.	Controversy on I. John, 5:7,	Criticus.
2186.	Converts' Manual,	A. Joy.
978.	Convict,	G. P. R. James.
221.	Cook's Voyages,	A. Kippis.

COOPER'S WORKS.

1408. Afloat and Ashore,
1409. Bravo.
1410. Chain Bearer.
1411. Deer-slayer.
1412. Headsman.
1413. Heidenmauer.
1414. Home as Found.
1415. Homeward Bound.
1416. Jack Tier.
1417. Last of the Mohicans.
1418. Lionel Lincoln.
4419. Monikins.
1420. Mercides of Castile.
1421. Miles Wallingford.
1422. Oak Openings.
1423. Pathfinder.
1424. Pilot.
1425. Pioneers.
1426. Precaution.
1427. Redskins.
1150. Red Rover.
1428. Red Rover.
1429. Satanstoe.
1430. Sea Lions.
1431. Spy.
1432. The Crater.
1433. The Prairie.
1434. Two Admirals.
1435. Water Witch.
1436. Ways of the Hour.
1437. Wing and Wing.
1438. Wept of Wish-ton-Wish.
1439. Wyandotte

No.	Title	Author
2041.	Corner Stone of Christian Truth,	Jacob Abbott.
1996.	Costumes and Personages in India,	Caleb Wright.
274.	Counsels to Young Men,	Eliphalet Nott.
1634.	Count Robert, of Paris,	Walter Scott.
1011.	Countess Gisella,	E. Marlitt.
1911.	Country Living and Thinking,	Gail Hamilton.
2117.	ditto ditto	ditto.

NO.	TITLE.	AUTHOR.
1001.	Country Neighborhood,	Miss E. A. Dupuy.
766.	Country Rambles in England.	
1197.	Courtesies of Wedded Life,	Mrs. Madeline Leslie.
1386.	Cousin Maude and Rosamond,	Mrs. M. J. Holmes.
1015.	Cousin Phillis,	Mrs. Gaskell.
1027.	Cradock Nowell,	Richard D. Blackmore.
1660.	Crayon Miscellany,	Washington Irving.
1196.	Crests from the Ocean World.	
317.	Criminal Trials,	Lady Duff Gordon.
172–3.	Cromwell's Letters and Speeches—2 Vols.,	Thomas Carlyle.
168–9.	Cromwell, Life of—2 Vols.,	M. Russell.
2020.	Cross and Crown,	M. J. McIntosh.
474.	Crusoe's Island, California and Washoe,	J. Ross Browne.
1214.	Cudjo's Cave,	J. T. Trowbridge,
467,	Culture Demanded by Modern Life,	E. L. Youmans.
1023.	Curates' Discipline,	Mrs. Eiloart.
804.	Curiosities of Crime,	James M. Levy.

CURTISS'S WORKS.

482.	Howadji in Syria.	483.	Potiphar Papers.
479.	Lotus Eating.	480.	Prue and I.
481.	Nile Notes.	1137.	Trumps.

323.	Cyclopedia of Wit and Humor,	William E. Burton.
1909.	Daily Monitor,	Charles Brooks.
1443–4.	Daisy Chain—2 Vols.	
1047.	Daisy Nichol,	Lady Hardy.
487.	Dale, Gen. Samuel, Life and Times of,	J. F. H. Claiborne.
994.	Daltons,	Charles Lever.
1044.	Dangerous Guest.	
1743.	Daniel Dickinson, Life, Letters, etc., Vol. 1,	J R. Dickinson.
975.	Daniel Dennison,	Mrs. Hofland.
993.	Darien,	Eliot Warburton.
1387.	Darkness and Daylight,	Mrs. M. J. Holmes.
1011.	Dark Nights' Work,	Mrs. Gaskell.

No.	TITLE.	AUTHOR.

DARWIN'S WORKS.

405–6. Descent of Man—2 Vols.
407. Emotions in Man and Animals.
408. Origin of Species.
409. Voyage Round the World.

No.	TITLE.	AUTHOR.
1270.	Daughter of an Empress,	Louisa Muhlbach.
1050.	Daughter of Heath,	William Black.
990.	Daughter of Night,	S. W. Fullom.
1465.	David Copperfield,	Charles Dickens.
1310–11.	ditto 2 Vols.,	ditto.
1533.	David Elginbrod,	George MacDonald.
1007.	Day's Ride,	Charles Lever.
1167.	Days of Shoddy,	Henry Morford.
1036.	Dead-Sea Fruit,	M. E. Braddon.
2067.	Death Bed Scenes,	Davis W. Clark.
441.	Decisive Battles of the World,	E. S. Creasy.
1146.	Deer-slayer,	J. Fennimore Cooper.
1411.	ditto	ditto.
385.	Democracy in America,	Alexis DeTocqueville.
277.	Demonology and Witchcraft,	Walter Scott
2250.	Demonstration of Man's Lost Estate,	J. Fletcher.
10.	Demosthenes on the Crown, etc.,	Charles R. Kennedy.
11.	Demosthenes' Phillipics, etc.,	ditto.
188–9.	Denmark, Sweden and Norway—2 Vols.,	A. Chrichton.
1018.	Denis Donne,	Annie Thomas.
1016.	Denis Duval,	William M. Thackeray.
1237.	De Profundus,	W. Gilbert.
966.	De Rohan,	Eugene Sue.
1787.	Derrick and Drill; or, Petroleum.	
405–6.	Descent of Man—2 Vols.,	Charles Darwin.
1477.	Deveraux,	Edward Lytton Bulwer.
953.	ditto	ditto.
802–3.	Diary of a Physician—2 Vols.	
1404.	Dickens, Charles, Life of, Vol. 1,	John Foster.
1405.	Dickens, Charles, Life of,	R. S. Mackenzie.
1406.	Dickens's Dictionary,	Gilbert A. Pierce.

NO. TITLE. AUTHOR.

DICKENS'S WORKS.

1305–6. Barnaby Rudge—2 Vols.
1462. Barnaby Rudge.
1307–8. Bleak House—2 Vols.
1463. Bleak House.
1309. Christmas Books.
1464. Christmas Stories.
1310-11. David Copperfield, 2 vols.
1465. David Copperfield.
1312-13. Dombey & Son—2 vols
1466. Dombey & Son.
1314. Edwin Drood.
1315. Great Expectations.
1471. Great Expectations.
1474. Hard Times.
1316. History of England.
1317–18. Little Dorrit—2 Vols.
1467. Little Dorrit, etc.
1319–20. Martin Chuzzlewit, 2 V.
1468. Martin Chuzzlewit.
1221–22. Nicholas Nickelby, 2 V.
1469. Nicholas Nickelby.
1323–4. Old Curiosity Shop, 2 V.
1470. Old Cruriosity Shop.
1325. Oliver Twist.
1471. Oliver Twist.
1326–7. Our Mutual Friend, 2 V.
1472. Our Mutual Friend.
1328. Pickwick Papers—2 Vols.
1473. Pickwick Papers.
1330. Pictures from Italy.
1331. Sketches by Boz.
1332. Tale of Two Cities.
1474. Tale of Two Cities, etc.
1333. Uncommercial Traveler.

No.	Title	Author
981.	Discipline of Life.	
2166.	Discourses on Happiness,	Agenor d'Gasparin.
2089.	Discourses on Nature of Religion,	Orville Dewey.
2090.	ditto ditto (2 Series,)	ditto.
2057.	Discourses on Doctrines of Christianity,	William G. Elliot.
485.	Discoveries at Ninevah,	A. H. Layard.
212.	Discovery of Northern Coast of America,	Patrick F. Tytler.
282.	Disordered Mental Action,	Thomas C. Upham.
1478.	Disowned,	Edward Lytton Bulwer.
953.	ditto	ditto.

D'ISRAELI'S NOVELS AND TALES.

1624. Alroy.
1626. Contrarine Flemming.
1628. Ixion.
1624. Sybil.
1626. Venetia.
1625. Conningsby.
1627. Henrietta Temple.
1629. Lothair.
1627. Tancred.
1628. Vivian Grey.

No.	TITLE.	AUTHOR.
305.	Distinguished Females,	An American Lady.
891.	ditto	ditto.
1885.	District School, As It Was,	Warren Burton.
1518.	Divine Comedy,	Dante.
1993.	Divine Providence,	Emanuel Swedenborg.
2150.	Divine Trinity, Letters on,	B. F. Barrett.
998.	Dodd Family Abroad,	Charles Lever.
1254.	Doctor's Daughter,	Sophie May.
2086.	Doctor Grant and the Nestorians,	Thomas Laurie.
1267.	Doctor Vandyke,	John E. Cooke.
1056.	Doctor Wainwright's Patient,	Edmund Yates.
1110.	Doctor Wilmer's Love,	Margaret Lee.
1143.	Doesticks,	Philander Doesticks.
1312–13.	Dombey and Son—2 Vols.,	Charles Dickens.
1466.	ditto	ditto.
477.	Don Quixotte,	Saavedra Cervantes.
1388.	Dora Deane,	Mrs. M. J. Holmes.
2184.	Double Witness of the Church,	William J. Kip.
787.	Dovecote.	
1839.	Down in Tennessee,	Edmund Kirke.
1801.	Downwards and Upwards.	

DRAPER'S WORKS.

373. Civil Policy of America.
326-8. Civil War in America—3 Vols.
365. Intellectual Developement of Europe.
366. Human Physiology.

No.	TITLE.	AUTHOR.
1051.	Durnton Abbey,	Thomas Adolphus Trollope.
1047.	Earls Dene.	R. E. Franchillon.
511.	Early Indiana, Trials and Sketches,	O. H Smith.
1105.	Easy Nat; or, The Three Apprentices,	A. L. Stimpson.
37.	Eaton, William, Life of,	Cornelius C. Felton.
1162.	Ebb Tide, and Other Stories,	Christian Reid.
1109.	Ebony Idol.	

NO.	TITLE.	AUTHOR.
1824.	Ecce Cœlum,	A Connecticut Pastor.
2160.	Ecce Deus.	
218.	Economy of Health,	James Johnson.
2099.	Economy Salvation,	Mrs. Phœbe Palmer.
1257.	Edelweiss,	Berthold Auerbach.
1258.	ditto	ditto.
1222.	Edgar Clifton,	C. Adams.

EDGEWORTH'S NOVELS.

1346.	Castle Rackrent, etc.,	Vol. 1.
1347.	Angelina, etc.,	" 2.
1348.	Murad, The Unlucky, etc.,	" 3.
1349.	Tales of Fashionable Life, etc.,	" 4.
1350.	The Absentee, etc.,	" 5.
1351.	Belinda,	" 6.
1352.	Leonora, etc.,	" 7.
1353.	Patronage, etc.,	" 8.
1354.	Harrington, etc.,	" 9.
1355.	Helen, etc.,	" 10.

1389.	Edna Browning,	Mrs. M. J. Holmes.
1822.	Education: Intellectual, Moral and Physical,	Herbert Spencer.
716–18.	Educational Report (Mass.)—3 Vols., 1861–8–9.	
36.	Edwards, Johnathan, Life of,	Samuel Miller.
1194.	Edwin Brothertoft,	Theodore Winthrop
1314.	Edwin Drood,	Charles Dickens.
611.	Egypt: Past and Present,	Joseph B Thompson.
976.	Ehrenstein,	G. P. R. James.
1797.	Electricity, Wonders of,	J. Baile.
2062.	Elegant Narratives.	
1013	Eleanor's Victory,	M. E. Braddon.
450.	El Gringo,	W. W. H. Davis.
1144.	Elia; or, Spain Fifty Years Ago,	Fernan Caballero.
33.	Eliot, John, Life of,	Convers Francis.

No.	TITLE.	AUTHOR.

ELIOT'S NOVELS.

1398. Adam Bede.
1399. Felix Holt.
1400. Romula.
1401. Silas Marner and Clerical Life.
1402. The Mill on the Floss.

No.	Title	Author
1582.	Elmwood.	
34.	Ellery, William, Life of,	Edward T. Channing.
303.	Eloquence, Principles of,	Abbe Maury.
1719.	Emancipation in the West Indies,	Mary A. Collier.
545.	Embassy to Eastern Courts,	Edmund Roberts.
972.	Emilia Wyndham.	
1203.	Emily Chester.	
550.	Eminent Americans,	Benson J. Lossing.
407.	Emotions of Man and Animals,	Charles Darwin.
132.	Empress Josephine,	John S. Memes.
885.	ditto	ditto.
1269.	Empress Josephine,	Louisa Muhlbach.
1207.	End of the World,	Edward Eggleston.
655-6.	England and the English—2 Vols.,	E. L. Bulwer.
627-8.	England, Condition and Fate of—2 Vols.	
1586.	English Literature,	Charles D. Cleveland.
1390.	English Orphans,	Mrs. M. J. Holmes.
1575.	Enigmas of Life,	W. R. Gray.
2200.	Entire Holiness,	John H. Wallace.
1736.	Episcopalianism,	B. F. Barrett.
459.	Episodes of French History,	Miss Pardoe.
1242.	Ernest Linwood,	Caroline L. Hunt.
955	Ernest Maltravers,	Edward Lytton Bulwer.
1480.	ditto	ditto.
1337.	Esmond and Barry Lynden,	William M. Thackeray.
1184.	Esperance,	Meta Lander.
383.	Essays,	Lord Macaulay.
2209.	Essays on Church of England,	Thomas T. Biddulph.
1044.	Estell Russell.	
29.	Ethan Allen,	Jared Sparks.
1391.	Ethelyn's Mistake,	Mrs. M. J. Holmes.
1392.	ditto	ditto.

NO.	TITLE.	AUTHOR.
1479.	Eugene Aram,	Edward Lytton Bulwer.
954.	ditto	ditto.
12–13.	Euripides' Tragedies—2 Vols.,	Theodore A. Buckley.
403–4.	European Morals—2 Vols.,	William E. H. Lecky.
1268.	Eustace Diamonds,	Anthony Trollope.
1003.	Evelyn Marston,	Mrs. Marsh.
2088.	Evenings with John Bunyan,	James Large.
694.	Every Saturday, (1866)—Vol. 1.	
694½.	ditto (1866)— " 2.	
676.	ditto (1871)— " 3.	
677.	ditto (1871)— " 3.	
1834.	Expanse of Heaven,	R. A. Proctor.
157–8.	Expedition Down the Niger—2 Vols.,	Richard Lander.
62.	Expedition to Borneo,	Henry Keppel.
145–6.	Expedition to the Pacific, (1804)—2 Vols.,	Paul Allen.
159–60.	Expedition to Russia—2 Vols.,	Phillip DeSegur.
376.	Expedition to the Zambezi,	David and Charles Livingstone.
2072.	Experience of a Layman,	Lyman Abbott.
541.	Exploration in Equatorial Africa,	Paul B. DuChaillu.
603.	Exploring Beyond the Rocky Mountains,	Samuel Parker.
1916	Eyes and Ears,	Henry Ward Beecher.
1213.	Fabrics: A Story of To-Day.	
1635.	Fair Maid of Perth,	Walter Scott.
1732–3	Fair of LaFontaine—2 Vols.,	Eliza Wright.
1052.	Fair to See,	L. W. M. Lockhart.
2231.	Faith Explained,	Charles Walker.
993.	Falkenburg.	
1039.	False Colors,	Annie Thomas.
957.	False Heir,	G. P. R. James.
2077.	Family and Closet Devotions.	
235.	Family Instructor.	
1577.	Farm Drainage,	Henry F. French.
1893.	Farmer and Gardener,	Thomas G. Fessenden.
194–5.	Farmers' Instructor—2 Vols.,	J. Buel.
2206.	Father Brighthopes,	Paul Crayton.
974.	Father Darcy,	Mrs. Marsh.
2063.	Father Henson's Story,	Mrs. Harriet Beecher Stowe.
1191.	Faustina,	Countess Hahn-Hahn.

No.	TITLE.	AUTHOR.
1399.	Felix Holt,	George Eliot.
1024.	ditto	ditto.
2183.	Fellowship with Christ,	Stephen H. Tyng.
972.	Female Minister.	
151–2.	Female Sovereigns—2 Vols.,	Mrs. Jameson.
1048.	Fenton's Quest,	M. E. Braddon.
394–6.	Ferdinand and Isabella—3 Vols.,	William H. Prescott.
1176	Fernando DeLemos,	Charles Gayarre.
1596.	Fern Leaves,	Fanny Fern.
1597.	ditto	ditto.
295.	Festivals and Amusements,	Horatio Smith.
793.	Festivals and Fasts of Protestant Episcopal Church,	John H. Hobert.
320–21.	Field Book of the Revolution—2 Vols ,	B. J. Lossing.
322.	Field Book of the War of 1812,	ditto.
1502.	Fielding's Works,	Henry Fielding.
363.	ditto	David Herbert.
1862.	Figurative Language,	David N. Lord.
1939.	Financial Policy During the Rebellion,	Simeon Newcomb.
1796.	Fireside Science,	James R. Nichols.
1611.	First Causes of Character,	Woodbury M. Fernald.
1010.	First Friendship.	
1710.	Five Gateways of Knowledge,	George Wilson.
1034.	Five Hundred Pounds Reward,	A Barrister.
1778.	Five Weeks in a Balloon,	William Lockland.
992.	Florence Sackville,	Mrs. Burbury.
1920.	Flower Garden,	Charlotte Elizabeth.
83.	Flowers of Fable.	C. K. F.
1453.	Folle Farine,	"Ouida."
1828.	Foods,	Edward Smith.
2097.	Footfalls on Boundary of Another World,	Robert D. Owen.
2152.	Foregleams of Immortality,	Edmund H. Sears.
864.	Foreign Conspiracy Against the United States.	
956.	Forest Days,	G. P. R. James.
1240.	Forest House and Catherine's Lovers,	Erckmann-Chatrian.
1050.	For Lack of Gold,	Charles Gibbon.
426.	Forms of Water,	John Tyndall
1056.	For the King,	Charles Gibbon

NO.	TITLE.	AUTHOR.
975.	Fortescue,	James Sheridan Knowles.
1636.	Fortunes of Nigel,	Walter Scott.
1003.	Fortunes of Glencore,	Charles Lever.
969.	Foster Brother,	Leigh Hunt.
1263.	Foul Play,	Charles Reade.
1039.	Found Dead,	James Payn.
1811.	Four Years in Yale,	Graduate of 1869.
421.	Fragments of Science,	John Tyndall.
668.	Franklin, Benjamin, Life of.	
1734.	Franklin's Life and Essays,	By Himself.
174–5.	Franklin, Benjamin, Memoirs of—2 Vols.	
1274.	Frederick The Great and His Court,	Louisa Mühlbach.
1273.	Frederick The Great and His Family,	Louisa Mühlbach.
2107.	Freedom of the Will,	D. D. Whedon.
595.	Frémont, John C., Life of, etc.,	John Bigelow.
1907.	Frémont, John C., Life and Exploration,	Charles W. Upham.
353–56.	French Revolution—4 Vols.,	A. Thiers.
1046.	From Thistles—Grapes,	Mrs. Eilôart.
1576.	Fruit, Flowers and Vegetables,	G. Emmerson.
38.	Fulton, Robert, Life of,	James Renwick.
1900.	Fun Better Than Physic,	W. W. Hall.
1202.	Gabriel Vane's Fortune and Friends,	Jeremy Loud.
1930.	Gala Days,	Gail Hamilton.
1264.	Galama,	J. B. DéLiefdè.
965.	Gambler's Wife,	Mrs. Grey.
2161.	Gates Ajar,	Elizabeth S. Phelps.
2037.	Gavazzi's Life and Lectures,	Father Gavazzi.
973.	Genevievé,	Alphonse Lamartine.
1779.	Genesis of Species,	St. George Mivart.
688.	Geography, Modern,	S. Augustus Mitchell.
700.	Geography, Pictorial,	S. G. Goodrich.
1875.	Geology, Elements of,	Samuel St. John.
265.	Geology, Elements of,	Charles A. Lee.
64.	George Canning, Life of,	Robert Bell.
496.	Georgia Scenes,	A Native Georgian.
1006.	Gerald Fitzgerald,	Charles Lever.
1256.	German Tales,	Berthold Aûerbach.
1023.	Gilbert Rugge.	

No.	TITLE.	AUTHOR.
1938.	Ginx's Baby.	
1877.	Glances at Europe,	Horace Greeley.
892.	Glen Cabin.	
2021.	God in His Providence,	W. M. Fernald.
1481.	Godolphin,	Edward Lytton Bulwer.
1058.	ditto	ditto.
701.	Godey's Lady's Book, Vol. 24—1842.	
702.	" " " " 25—1842.	
703.	" " " " 48—1854.	
704.	" " " " 49—1854.	
705.	" " " " 51—1855.	
706.	" " " " 52—1856.	
707.	" " " " 53—1856.	
1275.	Goethe and Schiller,	Louisa Mühlbach.
1922.	Gold Foil,	Timothy Titcomb.
990.	Gold Worshippers,	S. W. Fullom.
770.	Golden Christmas.	
2235.	Good Hope Through Grace,	Gardiner Spring.
2131.	Gospel in Ezekiel,	Thomas Guthrie.
980.	Gowrie,	G. P. R. James.
962.	Grandfather,	Miss Ellen Pickering.
2121.	Grandmother's Scrap Book.	
1175.	Granville De Vignè,	"Ouida."
551.	Grant and Sherman,	J. T. Headley.
1755.	Grasses and Forage Plants,	Charles L. Flint.
2119.	Graver Thoughts of a Country Parson.	
1315.	Great Expectations,	Charles Dickens.
982.	Great Hoggarty Diamond,	William M. Thackeray.
1339.	ditto ditto	ditto.
1856.	Great Red Dragon,	Anthony Gavin.
983.	Green Hand.	
1589.	Greenland, Observations and Adventures in,	Isaac I. Hayes.
1847.	Greenwood Leaves,	Grace Greenwood.
2004–5.	Grellet, Stephen, Life and Labors of—2 Vols.,	B. Seebohn.
1370.	Griffith Gaunt,	Charles Reade.
1123.	Grif. : A Story of Australian Life,	B. L. Farjeon.
1304.	ditto	ditto.
959.	Grumbler,	Miss Ellen Pickering

NO.	TITLE.	AUTHOR.
873.	Guide for Young Disciples,	J. G. Pike.
2221.	ditto ditto	ditto.
246.	Guide to Wisdom and Virtue.	
2228.	Guide to the Doubting,	Robert Phillip.
1033½.	Guild Court,	George MacDonald.
1294.	Guilt and Innocence,	Marie S. Schwartz.
1230.	Gustave Adolph and Thirty Years' War,	Z. Topelius.
1020.	Guy Deverell,	J. L. LèFanú.
1637.	Guy Mannering,	Walter Scott.
1043.	Gwendoline's Harvest,	James Payn.
2218	Hafed's Dream,	John Todd.
1228.	Hagar, The Martyr,	Mrs. H. M. Stevens.
1020.	Half a Million,	Amelia B. Edwards.
593,	Hamilton, Alexander, Life and Times of,	Samuel M. Smücker.
1020.	Hand and Glove,	Amelia B. Edwards.
791.	Hand-Book for Travellers on the Continent.	
281.	Hand-Book for Readers,	A. Potter.
985.	Hands—Not Hearts,	Janet W. Wilkinson.
1135.	Hannah,	Miss Mulock.
1205.	Hans Brinker: Story of Life in Holland,	Mary E. Dodge.
1723.	Happy Thoughts,	F. C. Burnard.
724.	Happy Home—Vols. 7–8,	William M. Thayer.
725.	Happy Home—Vol. 10,	William M. Thayer.
1000.	Hard Times,	Charles Dickens.
1482.	Harold,	Edward Lytton Bulwer.
980.	ditto	ditto.
905.	Harper's Magazine—Index Vols. 1 to 40.	
906.	Harper's Magazine, Volume 1 —1850.	
907–8.	" " " 2—3 —1851.	
909–10.	" " " 4—5 —1852.	
911–12.	" " " 6—7 —1853.	
913–14.	" " " 8—9 —1854.	
915–16.	" " " 10–11 —1855.	
917–18.	" " " 12–13 —1856.	
919–20.	" " " 14–15 —1857.	
921–22.	" " " 16–17 —1858.	
923–24.	" " " 18–19 —1859.	
925–26.	" " " 20–21 —1860.	

No.	TITLE.	AUTHOR.
927–28.	Harper's Magazine, Vols. 22–23 —1861.	
929-30.	" " " '24–25 —1862.	
931–32.	" " " 26–27 —1863.	
933–34.	" " " 28–29 —1864.	
935–36.	" " " 30–31 —1865.	
937–38.	" " " 32–33 —1866.	
939–40.	" " " 34–35 —1867.	
941–42.	" " " 36-37 —1868.	
943–44.	" " " 38–39 —1869.	
945–46.	" " " 40–41 —1870.	
947–48.	" " " 42–43 —1871.	
949–50.	" " " 44–45 —1872.	
951–52,	" " " 46–47 —1873.	
1182.	Harrington: Story of True Love,	Maria Edgeworth.
1944.	Harry and Lucy,	Maria Edgeworth.
1063.	Harry Heathcote,	Anthony Trollope.
2141.	Haynes, Rev. Lemuel, Life and Character,	T. M. Cooley
1412.	Headsman,	J. Fennimore Cooper.
993.	Head of the Family,	Miss Mulock.
1187.	ditto	ditto.
898.	Health Without Medicine,	L. B. Coles.
1638.	Heart of Midlothian,	Walter Scott.
1746–7.	Heart of Africa—2 Vols.,	George Schweinfurth.
1403.	Hearts Unveiled,	Sarah E. Saymore.
419.	Heat as a Mode of Motion,	John Tyndall.
2012.	Heaven and Hell,	Emanuel Swedenborg.
2026.	Heavenly Recognition,	H. Harbaugh.
1848.	Hawkins, John H. W.,	W. G. Hawkins.
1882.	ditto ditto	ditto.
1060.	"He Cometh Not," She Said,	Annie Thomas.
2148.	Hedged In,	Elizabeth S. Phelps.
974.	Heidelberg,	G. P. R. James.
1413.	Heidenmauer,	J. Fennimore Cooper.
1841.	Heights and Depths,	Agnes L. Scanland.
1002.	Heiress of Haughton,	Mrs. Marsh.
1045.	Heir Expectant.	
1627.	Henrietta Temple,	B. Disraeli.
644.	Henry Clay,	George D. Prentice.

NO.	TITLE.	AUTHOR
670.	Henry Clay,	George D. Prentice.
562.	Henry Clay, Monument to.	
995.	Henry Esmond,	William M. Thackeray.
989.	Henry Smeaton,	G. P. R. James.
1276.	Henry the Eighth and His Court,	Louisa Mühlbach.
960.	Heretic,	Lajétchnikoff.
8.	Herodotus,	Henry Carrey.
28.	Hero, and Other Tales,	Miss Mulock.
2185.	Heroes for The Truth,	K. W. Tweedie.
1062.	Her Face Was Her Fortune,	F. W. Robinson.
1049.	Her Lord and Master,	Florence Marryatt.
1038.	Hetty,	Henry Kingsley.
962.	H—— Family,	Frederika Bremer.
1210.	Hidden Path,	Marion Harland.
1147.	Higher Law.	
1041.	Hirell,	John Saunders.
198–200.	History, American, Tales from—3 Vols.	
606.	History, American, Incidents of,	J. W. Barber.
539.	History, Ancient,	M. E. Thalheimer.
248.	History, Beauties of, English,	J. Frost.
215.	History, Beauties of, French.	John Frost.
127.	History, Modern,	M. Michalet.
563.	History, Outlines of,	Marcius Willson.
68.	History for Boys,	John G. Edgar
505–6.	History of American Conflict—2 Vols.,	Horace Greeley.
289.	History of American Revolution,	J. L. Blake.
519.	History of American Socialisms,	John H. Noyes.
84.	History of Charlemágne,	G. P. R. James.
1994–5.	History of Christian Doctrine—2 Vols.,	K. R. Hagenbach.
245.	History of Connecticut,	Theodore Dwight.
568.	History of Decline and Fall of Roman Empire,	Edw. Gibbon.
236.	History of Discovery and Conquests of America,	W. Robertson.
347–9.	History of Dutch Republic—3 Vols.,	John L. Motley.
524–6.	History of Dutch Republic—3 Vols.,	ditto.
299.	History of Education,	H. I. Schmidt.
380–1.	History of England—2 Vols.,	Lord Macaulay.
1316.	History of England,	Charles Dickens.
569.	History of England,	David Hume.

No.	TITLE.	AUTHOR.
615.	History of England,	Mrs. Markham.
1–5.	History of England—5 Vols.,	Thomas B. Macaulay.
96–100.	History of England—5 Vols.,	Thomas Keightley.
572–83.	History of England—12 Vols.,	James A. Froude.
333–40.	History of Europe—8 Vols.,	Archibald Alison.
368–9.	History of France—2 Vols.,	M. Michelet.
570.	History of France (Illustrated).	
40–2.	History of France—3 Vols.,	Eyre C. Crowe.
240.	History of Fine Arts,	Benson J. Lossing.
625.	History of First Regiment Maryland Infantry, etc.,	C. Camper.
230.	History of Greece,	Oliver Goldsmith.
571.	History of Greece,	William Smith.
558.	History of Hartford Convention,	Theodore Dwight.
552.	History of Harvard University,	Benjamin Pierce.
589.	History of Illinois,	Thomas Ford.
60.	History of Italian Republics,	J. C. L. DeSimondi.
503.	History of Ireland,	Abbé MacGeoghegan.
667.	History of King Phillip's War,	Thomas Church.
283.	History of Louisiana,	E. Bunner.
292.	History of Michigan,	James H. Lannan.
116–7.	History of Massachusetts—2 Vols.,	Uncle Philip.
2101–2.	History of M. E. Church—2 Vols.,	Abel Stevens.
637.	History of Norman Conquest—Vol. 1,	Augustian Thierry.
518.	History of New England,	Hannah Adams.
196–7.	History of New Hampshire—2 Vols.,	Uncle Philip.
120-1.	History of New York—2 Vols.,	William Dunlap.
504–5.	History of Ohio in the War—2 Vols.,	Whitelaw Reid.
561.	History of 112th Regiment N. Y. Vols.,	William Hyde.
261.	History of Palestine,	Michael Russell.
1338.	History of Pendennis,	William M. Thackeray.
1381.	ditto ditto	ditto.
488.	History of Peninsula War,	C. William Vane.
134.	History of Persia,	James P. Frazier.
252.	History of Polynesia,	M. Russell.
225.	History of Poland,	James Fletcher.
661.	History of Pyrrhus,	Jacob Abbott.
2227.	History of Redemption,	President Edwards.
128.	History of Reign of Charles V.,	William Robertson.

NO.	TITLE.	AUTHOR.
878–82.	History of Rome—5 Vols.,	Titus Livius.
296.	History of Rome,	Oliver Goldsmith.
567.	History of Rome,	Henry G. Liddell.
800.	History of Spain, Pictures from.	
43–7.	History of Spain and Portugal—5 Vols.	
588.	History of Scandinavia,	Paul C. Linding.
640.	History of Scotland,	P. F. Tylter.
643.	History of South America and Mexico.	
79.	History of Switzerland.	
58.	History of Thirty Years' War,	Frederick Schiller.
520–3.	History of United Netherlands—4 Vols.,	John L. Motley.
170–1.	History of United States—2 Vols.,	Selma Hale.
639.	History of United States,	Emma Williard.
616.	History of United States,	G. P. Quackenbos.
617.	ditto ditto	ditto.
310.	History of Virginia,	Uncle Philip.
544.	History of Wisconsin (Military),	E. B. Quiner.
560.	History of Wisconsin, part 2d (Documentary),	W. R. Smith.
455–7.	History of the Girondists—3 Vols.,	A. De Lamartine.
630.	History of the Hen Fever,	George P. Barnham.
131.	History of the Moors of Spain,	M. Florian.
789.	History of the Rebellion (Youth's),	William M. Thayer.
2124–26.	History of the Reformation—3 Vols.,	J. H. M. d'Auibignè.
129.	History of the Roman Republics,	Adam Ferguson.
510.	History of the States.	
101–6.	History of the World—6 Vols.,	Alexander F. Tytler.
107–9.	History of the World (Sacred),—3 Vols.,	Sharon Turner.
532–3.	History of the War—1st and 2d year—(Southern) 2 Vols.,	Edward H. Pollard.
547.	Historical Collections of Massachusetts,	John W. Barber.
1870.	Historical, Literary, and Political Miscellany,	J. B. Cobb.
2194.	Historical Sketches of Striking Events,	D. W. Clark.
1106.	Hitherto: Story of Yesterday,	Mrs. A. D. T. Whitney.

HOLMES' WORKS.

1385. Cameron Pride.
1386. Cousin Maude and Rosamond.
1387. Darkness and Daylight.
1392. Ethelyn's Mistake.
1393. Homestead on the Hillside.
1394. Marian Grey.

No.	TITLE.	AUTHOR.
1388.	Dora Deane.	
1389.	Edna Browning.	
1390.	English Orphans.	
1391.	Ethelyn's Mistake.	
1395.	Meadow Brook.	
1396.	Rose Mather.	
1397.	Tempest and Sunshine.	

2156.	Holy Living and Dying,	Jeremy Taylor.
6.	Homer's Iliad,—Translated by,	Theodore A. Buckley.
7.	Homer's Odyssey, ditto	ditto.
1414.	Home as Found,	J. Fennimore Cooper.
27.	Home Influence,	Grace Aguilar.
2093.	ditto	ditto.
2019.	Home Life,	Elizabeth M. Sewell.
1783.	Home Pastimes,	J. H. Head.
2092.	Home Scenes,	Grace Aguilar.
1415.	Homeward Bound,	J. Fennimore Cooper.
1393.	Homestead on the Hillside,	Mrs. M. J. Holmes.
2085.	Homilatics,	Daniel P. Kidder.
1055.	Hope Deferred,	Eliza F. Pollard.
1415.	Hoosier School-Master,	Edward Eggleston.
598.	Horace Greeley, Life of,	James Parton.
599.	ditto ditto	ditto.
19.	Horace, Works of,	C. Smart.
362.	Horse-Doctor—Illustrated,	Edward Mayhew.
1059.	Hour and the Man,	Harriet Martineau.
420.	Hours of Exercise in the Alps,	John Tyndall.
2001.	Hours With the Evangelists—Vol. 1,	I. Nichols.
1154.	House by the Churchyard,	L. LèFanú.
1299.	House of York,	M. A. T.
1897.	Household Narratives.	
482.	Howadji in Syria,	George W. Curtiss.
1174.	How Could He Help It?	A. S. Roe.
1708.	How to Do It,	Edward E. Hale.
1823.	How to Make a Million,	Charles Léib.
886.	How to Observe the Golden Rule,	Emily Chubbück.
1816.	How the World Was Peopled,	Edward Fontaine.
38.	Hudson, Henry, Life of,	Henry C. Cleveland.
366.	Human Physiology,	John W. Draper.

NO.	TITLE.	AUTHOR
2115.	Humanity in the City,	E. H. Chapin.
237.	Humboldt's Travels,	W. Macguillivray.
1204.	Hunter's Feast,	Capt. Mayne Reid.
2116.	Hyacinthe, Father, Life and Discourses of,	Father Hyacinthe.
2211.	Hymns for Christian Devotion,	J. G. Adams.
306.	Iceland, Greenland, etc.	
470.	Ida Pfeiffer's Last Travels,	Ida Pfeiffer.
469.	Ida Pfeiffer's Second Journey Round the World,	Ida Pfeiffer
1451.	Idalia,	"Ouida."
1678.	If, Yes, and Perhaps,	Edward E. Hale.
2213.	Imitation of Christ,	Thomas A. Kempis.
901.	Important Questions,	James Smith.
136.	Improvement of Society,	Thomas Dick.
964.	Improvisitore,	Mary Howitt.
2140.	Incarnation, etc , of Jesus Christ,	Chauncey Giles.
1235.	India : The Pearl of Pearl River,	Mrs. E. D. E. N. Southworth.
88–9.	Indian Biography—2 Vols.,	B. B. Thatcher.
783.	Indian Fairy Book.	
535–6.	Indians, North American—2 Vols.,	George Catlin.
86–7.	Indian Traits—2 Vols.,	B. B. Thatcher.
1767.	Industries of the United States,	Horace Greeley, etc.
1045.	In Duty Bound.	
876.	Infidelity,	William Nevins.
1866.	Ingoldsby Legends,	Richard H. Barham.
1060.	Innocent,	Mrs. Oliphant.
1764.	Innocents Abroad,	Mark Twain.
1792.	Insects of North America,	B. Jæger.
1038.	In Silk Attire,	William Black.
849.	Instructions for Officers in Adjutant-General's Department.	
1852.	Insurrection *vs.* Resurrection in America,	A Virginian.
365.	Intellectual Development in Europe,	John W. Draper.
291.	Intellectual Powers,	John Abercrombie.
144–5.	Invasion of The Crimea—2 Vols.,	A. W. Kinglake.
649.	Irish in America,	John F. Maguire.
1724.	Irish Life,	W. Stewart French.
514.	Irving, Edward, Life of,	Mrs. Oliphant.

No.	TITLE.	AUTHOR.

IRVING'S WORKS.

1655. Alhambra.
1656. Astoria.
1657. Bonneville's Adventures.
1658. Bracebridge Hall.
1549. Bracebridge Hall.
1659. Conquests of Granada.
1660. Crayon Miscellany.
1661. Knickerbocker.
1662–4. Life and Voyages of Columbus—3 Vols.
1665–6. Mahomet and His Successors—2 Vols.
1667. Oliver Goldsmith.
1668. Salamagundi.
1669. Spanish Papers.
1670. Sketch Books.
1671. Tales of a Traveler.
1672. Wolfert's Roost.

No.	Title	Author
767.	Isaac Hopper,	L. Maria Child.
313.	Isabel; or, Trials of The Heart.	
777.	Italian Sketch Book,	An American.
142–4.	Italy and Italian Islands—3 Vols.,	William Spalding.
1639.	Ivanhoe,	Walter Scott.
994.	Ivar,	Miss Carlen.
1628.	Ixion,	B. Disraeli.
1356.	Jacob Faithful,	Captain Marryatt.
1416.	Jack Tier,	J. Fennimore Cooper.
675.	Jackson, Andrew, Life of.	
959.	Jack of the Mill,	William Howitt.
979.	Jane Eyre,	Currer Bell.
463.	Japan in Our Day,	Bayard Taylor.
254.	Japanese: Manners and Customs,	Von Siébold.
1357.	Japhet In Search of a Father,	Captain Marryatt.
1035.	Jeanie's Quiet Life.	
2241.	Jennison, Isaac, Memoirs of,	Edward Otherman
971.	Jessie's Flirtations.	
2260.	Jesus and The Woman of Sychar.	
2128.	Jesus, The Interpreter of Nature,	Thomas Hill.
1043.	John,	Mrs. Oliphant.
1748–9.	John, of Barneveld—2 Vols.,	John L. Motley.
1211.	John Guildersting's Sin.,	C. French Richards.
1200.	John Halifax,	Miss Mulock.
1003.	ditto	ditto.
1013.	John Marchmont,	M. E. Braddon.

NO.	TITLE.	AUTHOR.
50-1.	Jones, Paul, Life of—2 Vols.,	A. S. Mackenzie.
1460.	Joseph Andrews,	Henry Fielding.
1162.	Joseph And His Friend,	Bayard Taylor.
1062.	Joseph, The Jew.	
1277.	Joseph The Second and His Court	Louisa Mühlbach.
1051.	Joshua Marvel.	B. L. Farjeôn.
63.	Journey to Ararat.	Frederick Parrot.
471.	Journey Round The World,	F. Gerstæckér.
987.	Julia Howard,	Mrs. Martin Bell.
508.	Julius Cæsar—Vol. 1,	Louis Napoleon.
23.	Juvenal Persius,	Lewis Evans.
290.	Juvenile Companion, etc.,	J. L. Blake.
1209.	Kate Weston,	Jennie De Witt.
2049.	Kathagan Slave, etc.,	Emily Judson.
1038.	Kathaleen.	
996.	Katie Stewart,	Mrs. Oliphant.
1608.	Kavanagh,	Henry W. Longfellow.
273.	Keeping House and House Keeping,	Mrs. Sarah J. Hale.
2251.	Keeping the Heart,	John Flavell.
1113.	Kenelm Chillingly,	Edward Lytton Bulwer.
1135.	ditto	ditto.
1640.	Kenilworth,	Walter Scott.
1043.	Kilmeny,	William Black.
1769.	King, Hon. Rufus R., Addresses on Death of (in Congress.)	
1358.	King's Own,	Captain Marryatt.
1025.	Kissing The Rod,	Edmund Yates.
1621.	Kit Carson, Life of,	Charles Bardett.
1040.	Kitty,	M. Betham Edwards.
1661.	Knickerbocker,	Washington Irving.
755.	Knickerbocker—Vol. 2,	Washington Irving.
638.	Knightly Soldier,	H. C. Trumbull.
1901.	Know The Truth,	J. H. Jones.
2238.	Knox, John,	Ernest Renan.
763.	Kossuth and His Generals,	Henry W. DePûy.
1015.	Ladder of Life,	Amelia B. Edwards.
732.	Ladies' Garland, (1841).	
991.	Lady And The Priest,	Mrs. Maberly.
2061.	Lady Huntington And Her Friends,	Mrs. H. C. Kneight.

No.	TITLE.	AUTHOR.
998.	Lady Lee's Widowhood.	
1303.	Lady of Lyndon,	Lady Blake.
969.	Lady of Milan,	Mrs. Thomson.
671.	Lafayette, Life of.	
764.	Laird of Norlaw.	
465.	Lake Regions of Central Africa,	Bayard Taylor.
1292.	Lakeville,	Mary Healy.
370.	La Platá,	Thomas J. Page.
954.	Last Days of Pompeii,	Edward Lytton Bulwer.
1483.	ditto	ditto
1484.	Last of The Barons,	Edward Lytton Bulwer.
956.	ditto	ditto.
979.	Last of The Fairies,	G. P. R. James.
1417.	Last of The Mohicans,	J. Fennimore Cooper.
1741.	Lawrence, Amos, Diary and Correspondence of,	William R. Lawrence.
424.	Lectures In America,	John Tyndall.
1641.	Legend of Montrose,	Walter Scott.
1058.	Leila,	Edward Lytton Bulwer.

LAMARTINE'S WORKS.

455–7. History of The Girondists—3 Vols.
436–8. Memoirs of Celebrated Characters—3 Vols.
491. Past, Present, and Future of the Republic.
492. Raphael; or, The Pages of The Book of Life at Twenty.
493. The Stone Mason.

LAMB'S WORKS.

427. Letters—Vol. 1
428. Letters—Vol. 2.
329. Essays—Vol. 3.
430. Essays, etc.—Vol. 4.
431. Essays, Letters—Vol. 5.

2079.	Lamps, Pitchers and Trumpets,	Edwin P. Hood.
2027–8.	Land and Book—2 Vols.,	William M. Thompson.
1024.	Land at Last,	Edmund Yates.
460.	Land of Thor,	J. Ross Browne.

NO.	TITLE.	AUTHOR.
1484½.	Land of Thor,	J. Ross Browne.
1004.	Leonora D'Orco,	G. P. R. James.
1740.	Leo The Tenth, Life and Times of.	
974.	Leotine,	Mrs. Maberly.
2192.	Lessons On The Liturgy,	A Churchman.
1808.	Letters Of A Traveler from Spain,	William Cullen Bryant.
2207.	Letters To A Sister,	Harvey Newcomb.
854.	Letters To A Very Young Lady.	
973.	Lettice Arnold,	Mrs. Marsh.
781.	Lewie; Or, The Bended Twig,	Cousin Cicely.
1234.	Lewell Pastures.	
963.	Líbussa,	J. H. Musæus.
612.	Life and Death in Rebel Prisons,	Robert H. Kellogg.
1006.	Life For a Life,	Miss Muloch.
345.	Life in Brazil,	Thomas Ewbank.
2230.	Life in Earnest.	
82.	Life in Prairie Lands,	Eliza W. Farnham.
1593.	Life in Varied Phases,	Mrs. C. H. Butler.
2242.	Life of Faith,	W. Romaine.
995.	Life of Vicissitudes,	G. P. R. James.
77.	Life Studies; Or, How to Live,	John Baillie.
2136.	Life Thoughts,	Henry Ward Beecher.
2083.	Life's Lessons.	
1108.	Light,	Helen Modet.
425.	Light and Electricity,	John Tyndall.
2149.	Light In Darkness.	
2104.	Light On The Last Things,	William B. Hayden.
1131.	Like and Unlike,	A. S. Roe.
494.	Life in Santo Domingo,	A Settler.
527.	Lincoln, Abraham, Life of,	Ward H. Lamon.
528.	Lincoln, Abraham, Life of,	Henry J. Raymond.
769.	Linda; Or, The Young Pilot,	Caroline L. Hentz.
1418.	Lionel Lincoln,	J. Fennimore Cooper.
1104.	Lippincott's Gazetteer of the World,	J. B. Lippincott.
710–11.	Literature and Science—2 Vols.	
229-30.	Literature of Europe—2 Vols.,	Henry Hallam.
756.	Literary Miscellany—Vol. 3,	Willman.
1317–8.	Little Dorrit—2 Vols.,	Charles Dickens.

No.	TITLE.	AUTHOR.
1467.	Little Dorrit,	Charles Dickens.
1951.	Little Men,	Louisa M. Alcot.
1023.	Little Ragamuffin,	James Greenwood.
1949.	Little Women,	Louisa M. Alcot.
1950.	ditto	ditto.
262.	Live and Let Live.	
1012.	Live It Down,	J. C. Jeaffreason.
973.	Livonian Tales.	
234.	Lives and Voyages of Drake, Cavender, etc.	
618–9.	Lives of Eminent Men—2 Vols.	
553.	Lives of the Presidents,	Robert W. Lincoln.
1026.	Lizzie Lorton,	E. Lyman Lynton.
2036.	Lobdel, Henry, Memoir of,	W. S. Tyler.
1246.	Long Look Ahead,	A. S. Roe.
964.	Look to the End,	Mrs. Ellis.
1128.	Looking Around,	A. S. Roe.
1295.	Lord Kilgobbin,	Charles Lever.
2055.	Lord's Prayer, Lectures on,	William R. Williams.
1036.	Lost Name,	J. Sheridan Lè Fanú.

LORD LYTTON'S WORKS.

1475. Alice.
1476. Caxtons.
1477. Devereaux.
1478. Disowned.
1479. Eugene Aram.
1480. Ernest Maltravers.
1481. Godolphin.
1482. Harold.
1483. Last Days of Pompeii.
1484. Last of the Barons.
1484½. Leila.
1485. Lucretia.
1486–7. My Novel—2 Vols.
1488. Night and Morning.
1489. Paul Clifford.
1490. Pelham.
1490½. Pilgrims of the Rhine.
1491. Rienzi.
1492. Strange Story.
1493–4. What Will He Do With It?—2 Vols.
1495. Zanoni.

No.	TITLE.	AUTHOR.
782.	Loss of Brig Commerce—Suffering of Crew,	Capt. Jas. Riley.
1158.	Lost and Saved,	Mrs. Norton.
1159.	ditto,	ditto.
509.	Lost Cause,	Edward A. Pollard.

NO.	TITLE.	AUTHOR.
231.	Lost Greenland,	Uncle Philip
1243.	Lost Heir of Linlitchgow,	Mrs. E. D. E. N. Southworth.
957.	Lost Ship,	Capt. Neale.
1133.	Lothair,	B. Disraeli.
1112.	ditto,	ditto.
1629.	ditto,	ditto.
1063.	Lottie Darling,	John Cordy Jeaffreason.
479.	Lotus Eating,	George W. Curtiss.
451-2.	Louis XIV and Court of France—2 Vols,	Miss Pardôe.
1278.	Louisa of Prussia and Her Times,	Louisa Mühlbach.
969.	Love and Mesmerism,	Horace Smith.
2082.	Love L'Amour,	M. J. Mitchelet.
1372.	Love Me Little, Love Me Long,	Charles Reade.
1036	Love Or Marriage,	William Black.
276.	Love Token for Children.	
1017.	Lovel the Widower,	William M. Thackeray.
1051.	Lovels of Arden,	M. E. Braddon.
997.	Lover's Stratagem,	Emilie Flygare Carlen.
1183.	Lucia: Her Problem,	Amanda M. Douglass.
1133.	Luck of Roaring Camp,	Bret Harte.
1485.	Lucretia,	Lord Lytton.
974.	ditto,	ditto.
35.	Lucretia M. Davidson, Life of	
2179 & 95.	Luther, Martin, Life and Times of,	Geo. Cobbitt.
988.	Lutrells,	Folkstone Williams.
1033.	Mabel's Progress.	
760.	Mabel Vaughn.	
440.	Madeira, Portugal and the Andalusias of Spain.	
1953.	Madam Guyon's Letters,	P. L. Upham.
1107.	Madge; Or, Night and Morning,	H. B. G.
1027.	Madonna Mary,	Mrs. Oliphant.
2208.	Magdalen Churchyard,	J. J. Regnault Warin.
1845.	Magic Staff,	Andrew J. Davis.
748.	Magnolia, Or, Friendship's Gift,	Mrs. M. O. Stephens.
1665-6.	Mahomet and His Successors—2 Vols.,	Washington Irving.
964.	Maid of Honor.	
986.	Maid of Orleans.	
1055.	Maid of Sker,	R. D. Blackman.

No.	TITLE.	AUTHOR.
1188.	Marjorie's Quest,	Jeanie T. Gould.
1170.	Major Jone's Courtship,	Major Jones.
384.	Malay Archipelago,	Alfred R. Wallace.
1936.	Manderville—Vol. 1,	William Godwin.
1777.	Man and His Dwelling Place,	James Hinton.
2103.	Man As a Spiritual Being,	Chauncey Giles.
2163.	Man In Earnest,	Robert Collier.
472–3.	Mardi, And a Voyage Thither—2 Vols.,	Herman Melville.
1591.	Marble Prophecy,	J. G. Holland.
1247.	Margaret,	Sylvester Judd.
1016.	Margaret Denzil.	
978.	Margaret Graham,	G. P. R. James.
1033½.	Margaret's Engagement.	
489.	Marlborough, Life of,	Archibald Alison.
1871.	Mark Twain,	Autobiography.
894.	Maria Cheeseman; Or, The Candy Girl.	
1579.	Marie Antoinette and Her Son,	Louisa Mühlbach.
672.	Marion, General, Life of.	
1394.	Marion Grey,	Mrs. M. J. Holmes.
38.	Marquette, Jacques, Life of,	Jared Sparks.
916.	Marriage,	Miss Ferrier.
1161.	Married Belle,	Julia P. Smith.
977.	Martins of Chro Martin,	Charles Léver.
1319–20.	Martin Chuzzlewit—2 Vols.,	Charles Dickens.
1287.	ditto,	ditto.
1468.	ditto,	ditto.
1012.	Master Pole,	John Saunders.
596–7.	Marryatt, Captain, Life and Times of,	Florence Marryatt.

MARRYATT'S WORKS.

1356. Jacob Faithful.
1357. Japhet In Search of a Father.
1358. King's Own.
1359. Midshipman Easy.
1360. Naval Officer.
1361. Newton Foster.
1362. Pacha of Many Tales.
1363. Percival Keene.
1364. Peter Simple.
1365. Phantom Ship.
1366. Snarleyow.
1367. The Poacher.

NO.	TITLE.	AUTHOR.
1012.	Mary Lindsay,	Lady Emily Ponsonby.
981.	Mary Barton,	Mrs. Gaskill.
147-8.	Mary Queen of Scots—2 Vols.,	Henry G. Bell.
2073.	Masonry and Religion,	Charles Scott.
350-1.	Massachusetts In The Civil War—2 Vols.,	William Schouler.
352.	Massachusetts In The Rebellion,	P. C. Headley.
846.	Massachusetts Gazetteer (1828),	Jeremiah Spofford.
749.	Massachusetts Teacher, Volume 1,	1848.
750.	" " " 2,	1849.
751.	" " " 3,	1850.
752.	" " " 4,	1851.
1236.	Match Girl.	
34.	Mather, Cotton, Life of,	William B. O. Peabody.
1139.	Matrimonial Infelicities, &c,	Barry Grey.
1017.	Mattie—A Stray.	
1053.	Maud Mohen,	Annie Thomas.
1164.	Maurice,	Frédèric Béchard
1016.	Maurice Dering,	George A. Lawrence.
992.	Maurice Tiernay,	Charles Lever.
1239.	Mauprat,	George Sand.
1022.	Maxwell Drewitt,	F. G. Trafford.
1686.	May, Samuel J., Life of,	George B. Emerson.
1395.	Meadow Brook,	Mrs. M. J. Holmes.
243.	Means and Ends of Self Training.	
255.	Mechanics, Application of,	James Renwick.
251.	Mechanics, Illustrations of,	H. Maseley.
685-6.	Medical and Surgical History of the Rebellion (1861)—2 Vols.,	Surgeon-General U. S. Army.
2147.	Meditations on Life and Duties,	Zschokke.
436-8.	Memoirs of Celebrated Characters—3 Vols.,	A. De Lamartine.
178-9.	Men of Modern Times—2 Vols.	
1781.	Mental Physiology,	William B. Carpenter.
1420.	Mercedes of Castile,	J Fennimore Cooper.
1280.	Merchant of Berlin,	Louisa Mühlbach.
263.	Messopotamia and Assyria,	J. Baillie Fraser.
1039.	Meta's Faith.	
651.	Mexico; Its Peasants and Its Priests,	Robert A. Wilson.
1821.	ditto,	ditto.

No.	TITLE.	AUTHOR.
607.	Mexican War Reviewed,	William Jay.
608.	ditto,	ditto.
626.	Mexican War, Origin of, &c.,	Edward D. Mansfield.
423.	Michael Faraday,	John Tyndall.
332.	Middle Ages,	Henry Hallam.
982.	Midnight Sun,	Frederika Bremer.
1359.	Midshipman Easy,	Capt. Marryatt.
978.	Midsummers Eve,	Mrs. S. C. Hall.
1037.	Mildred,	Georgianna M. Craik.
1421.	Miles Wallingford,	J. Fennimore Cooper.
1007.	Mill On The Floss,	George Eliot.
1402.	ditto,	ditto.
1218.	Miller of Angibault,	George Sand.
1752.	Military and Civil Life,	William Hull.
1776.	Military Biography,	Charles C. Chesney.
719.	Military Road from Fort Walla-Walla, &c.,	J. Mullan.
1853.	Milwaukee Chronicles,	A. C. Wheeler.
1830.	Mind and Body,	Alexander Bain.
1040.	Minister's Wife,	Mrs. Oliphant.
1119.	Mirèio,	Frederic Mistral.
1886.	Mirror of Nature,	C. H. Schubert.
1019.	Miss Carew,	Amelia B. Edwards.
1018.	Miss Mackenzie,	Anthony Trollope.
1022.	Miss Majoribanks,	Mrs. Oliphant.
1215.	Miss Oona McQuarrie,	Alexander Smith.
1238.	Miss Roberts' Fortune,	Sophy Winthrop.
1772.	Mission Ridge and Lookout Mountain,	B. F. Taylor.
1557–9.	Miscellaneous Essays—3 Vols.,	Walter Scott.
382.	Miscellanies,	Lord Macaulay.
1106.	Misrepresentation,	Anna H. Drury.
1009.	Mistress and Maid,	Miss Muloch.
446–7.	Mitford, Mary Russell—2 Vols.,	A. G. K. Lestrang.
1574.	Moby Dick; Or, The Whale,	Herman Melville.
1729.	Model Young Man,	W. B. Sprague.
39.	Modern British Plutarch,	W. C. Taylor.
1855.	Modern Society,	Miss C. Sinclair.
884.	Mohammed, Life of,	George Bush.
1281.	Mohammed Ali and His House,	Louisa Mühlbach.

NO.	TITLE.	AUTHOR.
1048.	Monarch of Mincing Lane,	William Black.
29.	Montgomery, Richard,	John Armstrong.
1650.	Monastery,	Walter Scott.
1419.	Monikins,	J. Fennimore Cooper.
1248.	Monsieur Sylvester,	George Sand.
259.	Moral Feelings, Philosophy of,	John Ambercrombie.
2175.	Moral Lessons,	M. F. Cowdery.
2051.	Moral Science,	Francis Wayland.
897.	Moral Tales,	Peter Parley.
2201.	Moral Tales for the Young,	Mary Howitt.
52-3.	Moral Tales—2 Vols.,	Maria Edgeworth.
54-5.	Morality and Polity—2 Vols.,	William Whewell.
983.	Mordaunt Hall,	Mrs. Marsh.
1698.	Moran, James, Story of.	
1699.	Mormons, Fifteen Years Among,	Nelson W. Green.
605.	Mormons, History of.	
1892.	Mormonism, Its Leaders and Designs,	John Hyde, Jr.
1535.	Mormonism, Origin and Progress of,	Pomeroy Tucker.
768.	Morning Exercises for the Closet.	
1563.	Morning Star of the New World,	H. F. Parker.
1297.	Morton House,	Christian Reid.
1448.	Moss Side,	Marion Harland.
1000.	Mother's Recompense,	Grace Aguilar.
417.	Mountaineering In Sierra Nevada,	Clarence King.
2215.	Mount of Olives,	James Hamilton.
65.	Mozart, Life of,	Edward Holmes.
1675.	Mrs. Partington, Life and Sayings,	B. P. Shillaber.
1030.	Mr. Wynyard's Ward,	Holme Lee.

MUHLBACH'S WORKS.

1272. Andreas Hofer.
1271. Berlin and Sans Souci.
1270. Daughter of an Empress.
1269. Empress Josephine.
1273. Frederick The Great and his Family.
1274. Frederick The Great and his Court.
1275. Goethe and Schiller.

No.	TITLE.	AUTHOR.
1276.	Henry The Eighth and his Court.	
1277.	Joseph The Second and his Court.	
1278.	Louisa of Prussia and her Times.	
1279.	Marie Antoinette and her Son.	
1280.	Merchant of Berlin.	
1281.	Mohammed Ali and his House.	
1282.	Napoleon and Queen Louisa.	
1283.	Napoleon and the Queen of Prussia.	
1284.	ditto.	
1285.	Napoleon and Blucher.	
1286.	Old Fritz and New Era.	
1287.	ditto.	
1288.	Prince Eugene and his Times.	
1289.	Queen Hortense.	
1290.	ditto.	
1127.	Story of a Millionnaire.	
1498.	Two Life Paths.	

No.	TITLE.	AUTHOR.
1449.	Mysteries of Metropolisville,	Edward Egleston.
1600.	My Wife and I,	Harriet Beecher Stowe.
955.	Nabob at Home.	
1285.	Napoleon and Blucher,	Louisa Mühlbach.
1283.	Napoleon and Queen of Prussia,	Louisa Mühlbach.
1284.	ditto.	ditto.
1282.	Napoleon and Queen Louisa,	Louisa Mühlbach.
1151.	Nathalie,	Julia Kavanah.
830.	National Homes for Disabled Volunteers,	James Barber.
831.	ditto,	ditto.
220.	Nature, Beauties of, &c.,	Charles Bucke.
258.	Nature Laid Open,	J. L. Blacke.
280.	Nature, Observation of,	Robert Mudie.
1701.	Nature's Aristocracy,	Miss Jeannie Collins.
1037.	Nature's Noble Man.	
1842.	Natural History,	Sarah A. Myers.
1620.	Natural History,	Actaea.
234.	Natural History,	Uncle Philip.
1923.	Natural History,	A. Ackerman.

NO.	TITLE.	AUTHOR.
1937.	Natural History,	Oliver Goldsmith.
260.	Natural History of Birds.	
241.	Natural History of Elephants.	
176–7.	Natural History of Insects—2 Vols.	
308.	Natural History of Quadrupeds.	
242.	Natural History of Selborne,	Gilbert White.
204.	Natural History of Magic,	David Brewster.
219.	Natural Philosophy,	James Renwick.
1759.	Natural Philosophy,	Neil Arnott.
788.	Natural Philosophy,	Denison Olmstead.
1592.	Natural Philosophy,	J. L. Cumstock.
216.	Natural Philosophy, Illustrations of,	James Renwick.
182–3.	Natural Philosophy—2 Vols.,	Leonard Euler.
1918.	Natural Philosophy,	John W. Draper.
190–91.	Natural Theology—2 Vols.,	William Paley.
48.	Naturalists, Voyages of,	Charles Darwin.
49.	ditto,	ditto.
1360.	Naval Officer,	Captain Marryatt.
985.	Ned Allen,	David Hannay.
957.	Neighbors, (Novel),	Frederika Bremer.
298.	Nelson, Life of,	Robert Southey.
1375–6.	Never Too Late To Mend—2 Vols.,	Charles Reade.
1373.	ditto,	ditto.
1374.	ditto,	ditto.
1361.	Newton Foster,	Captain Marryatt.
288.	Newton, Sir Isaac, Life of,	David Brewster.
883.	ditto,	ditto.
648.	New Age of Gold,	Robert D. Romaine.
2154.	New Age and Its Messenger,	W. F. Evans.
1833.	New Chemistry,	J. P. Cooke, Jr.
2031.	New Church Doctrines,	S. Noble.
2025.	New Dispensation,	B. F. Barrett.
1059.	New Magdalen,	Wilkie Collins.
76.	New Spirit of the Age,	R. H. Harine.
2035.	New Testament, (new translation),	Leicester A. Sawyer.
1321–2.	Nicholas Nickleby—2 Vols.,	Charles Dickens.
1469	ditto,	ditto.
986.	Night and Morning,	Edward Bulwer Lytton.

No.	TITLE.	AUTHOR.
1488.	Night and Morning,	Edward Bulwer Lytton.
481.	Nile Notes,	George W. Curtiss.
367.	Ninevah and Babylon,	Austin H. Layard.
1227.	Noble Lord,	Mrs. E. D. E. N. Southworth.
1031.	No Man's Friend,	Frederick William Robinson.
1030.	Nora and Archibald Lee.	
977.	Norman's Bridge,	Mrs. Marsh.
1876.	Norwood; or, Village Life in New England,	H. W. Beecher.
1904.	North America,	Anthony Trollope.
1001.	North and South,	Mrs. Gaskell.
2045.	Notes from Plymouth Pulpit,	Henry Ward Beecher.
632.	Notes of Hospital Life.	
1004.	Nothing New,	Miss Muloch.
1008.	Notice to Quit,	W. G. Wills.
1186.	Now and Then,	Samuel Warren.
211.	Nubia and Abyssinia,	Michael Russell.
1422.	Oak Openings,	J. Fennimore Cooper.
1861.	Object Lessons, Manual of,	Marcius Wilson.
2157.	Object of Life.	
691–93.	Odd Fellows' Family Companion—Vols. 6–8–9.	
754.	Odd Fellows' Offering, (1846).	
504–5.	Ohio In The War of The Rebellion—2 Vols.,	Whitelaw Reid.
531.	Okavango River,	Charles J. Anderson.
775.	Old Brewery and Five Points' Mission,	Ladies of the Mission.
1323–4.	Old Curiosity Shop—2 Vols.,	Charles Dickens.
1471.	ditto,	ditto.
1002.	Old Dominion,	G. P. R. James.
1952.	Old Fashioned Girl,	Louisa M. Alcott.
1286.	Old Fritz and the New Era,	Louisa Mühlbach.
774.	Old Hicks, The Guide,	Charles W. Webber.
1118.	Old Homestead,	Mrs. A. S. Stephens.
1642.	Old Mortality,	Walter Scott.
987.	Old Oak Chest,	G. P. R. James.
1899.	Old Sights With New Eyes.	
2180.	Old South Chapel Prayer Meeting.	
2074.	Old Testament Legends,	S. Baring Gould.
1903.	Old Town Folks,	Mrs. H. B. Stowe.
1802.	Old World in a New Face—Vol. 2,	Henry W. Bellows

NO.	TITLE.	AUTHOR.
989.	Olive, (Novel,)	Miss Muloch.
1009.	Old Blake,	John Cordy Jeaffreason.
1667.	Oliver Goldsmith,	Washington Irving.
1325.	Oliver Twist,	Charles Dickens.
1471.	ditto,	ditto.
1055.	Ombra, (Novel,)	Mrs. Oliphant.
493.	Omoo: Adventures in South Seas,	Herman Melville.
1018.	On Guard,	Annie Thomas.
784.	One in a Thousand.	
1034.	One of the Family,	James Payn.
1007.	One of Them,	Charles Lever.
1220.	On the Heights,	Berthold Aûerbach.
968.	Only a Fiddler,	Andersen.
1041.	Only Herself,	Annie Thomas.
1121.	Opportunity,	Annie W. Crane.
74.	Orators of the Age,	G. H. Francis.
1813.	Orbs Around Us,	Richard A. Proctor.
343.	Oriental and Western Siberia,	T. W. Atkinson.
590.	Origin of the Late War, (1867),	George Lunt.
408.	Origin of Species,	Charles Darwin.
233.	Ornaments Discovered,	Mary Hughes.
1229.	Orpheus C. Kerr Papers,	O. C. Kerr.
968,	O. T., (Novel),	Hans Christian Anderson.
1818.	Other Worlds Than Ours,	R. A. Proctor.
1302.	Ought We To Visit Her?	Mrs. Annie Edwards.
2105.	Our Children In Heaven,	William H. Holcombe.
2196.	Our Eternal Homes,	Bible Student.
1863.	Our Girls,	Dio Lewis.
2176.	Our Happy Home,	Mrs. Sarah Gould.
1233.	Our Honey-Moon, &c.,	"Punch."
1326-7.	Our Mutual Friend—2 Vols.,	Charles Dickens.
1472.	ditto,	ditto.
458.	Our Rulers and Our Rights,	Anson Willis.
899.	Our Sympathizing High Priest.	
70.	Our Year (Child's Book).	
1910.	Out Of Door Papers,	Thomas W. Higginson.
1362.	Pacha of Many Tales,	Captain Marryatt.
2258.	Page, Harlan, Memoir of.	

No.	TITLE.	AUTHOR.
137–41.	Painters and Sculptors—5 Vols.,	Allan Cunningham.
746.	Pamphlets, Chicago Magazine, &c.	
720–3.	Panorama of Life and Literature—4 Vols.,	E. Littell.
902.	Panting After Holiness.	
1554.	Paris Commune,	W. Pembroke Fetridge.
1340.	Paris, Irish and Eastern Sketch Book,	W. M. Thackeray.
1382.	ditto,	ditto.
1793.	Paris Tricolored Sketches.	
1869.	Parisian Family,	Madame Guizot De Witt.
1896.	Parley's Present,	S. G. Goodrich.
967.	Parsonage of Mora,	Frederika Bremer.
1056.	Passion in Tatters,	Annie Thomas.
491.	Past, Present, and Future of the Republic,	A. De Lamartine.
2170.	Pastor's Testimony,	J. A. Clark.
1423.	Pathfinder,	J. Fennimore Cooper.
2153.	Patience of Hope,	John G. Whittier.
1514.	Patrick Henry,	William Wirt.
1052	Patty, (Novel),	Katharine S. Macquoid.
1489.	Paul Clifford,	Edward Bulwer Lytton.
953.	ditto,	ditto.
316.	Peasant Boy Philosopher,	Henry Mayhew
549.	Pedestrian Journey Through Russia, &c., (1820),	J. D. Cochrane.
972.	Peers and Parvenus,	Mrs. Gore.
1377.	Peg Woffington, &c.,	Charles Reade.
953.	Pelham,	Edward Bulwer Lytton.
1490.	ditto,	ditto.
601.	Peninsula Campaign,	J. J. Marks.
673.	Penn, William, Life of.	
1363.	Percival Keene,	Captain Marryatt.
268.	Perilous Adventures, &c.,	R. A. Davenport.
24 9.	Perils of the Sea.	
1458.	Peregrine Pickle,	T. Smollett.
1364.	Peter Simple,	Captain Marryatt.
126.	Peter The Great,	John Barrow.
1948.	Peter The Whaler,	William H. G. Kingston.
712.	Peterson's Magazine, (1852).	
988.	Petticoat Government,	Mrs. Trollope.

NO.	TITLE.	AUTHOR.
1643.	Peveril of the Peak,	Walter Scott.
994.	Pequinillo,	G. P. R, James.
186–7.	Perry, Commodore—2 Vols.,	Alexander S. Mackenzie.
1529.	Phantastes,	George Macdonald.
1530.	ditto,	ditto.
1365.	Phantom Ship,	Captain Marryatt.
1024.	Phemie Keller,	F. G. Trafford.
397–9.	Philip The Second—3 Vols.,	W. H. Prescott.
130.	Philosophers, Ancient, Lives of,	John Cormack.
114–15.	Philosophy, History of—2 Vols.,	C. S. Henry.
287.	Philosophy of Living,	Caleb Ticknan.
56–7.	Philosophy of Magic—2 Vols.,	Anthony T. Thompson.
1933–4.	Philosophy of Magic—2 Vols.,	Eusebe Salverte.
73.	Philosophy of Mystery,	Walter C. Dendy.
1791.	Philosophy of the Weather,	T. B. Butler.
34.	Phips, Sir William, Life of,	Francis Bowen.
1898.	Phrenology,	George Combe.
1917.	Phrenology, Lectures on,	ditto.
1765–6.	Phrenology, Annals of—2 Vols.	
1753–4.	Phrenology, Physiological, etc.—2 Vols.,	J. G. Spurzheim.
1744.	Phrenology, System of.	
1827.	Physics and Politics,	Walter Bagehot.
1731.	Physiology of Digestion,	Andrew Combe.
270.	Physiology, Principles of,	Andrew Combe.
1587.	Physicians Problems,	Charles Elam.
69.	Physical Sciences,	Mary Somerville.
1328–9.	Pickwick Papers—2 Vols.,	Charles Dickens.
1473.	ditto,	ditto.
1987.	Pictorial National Library—Vol. 3.	
1177.	Picture from Last Century,	Talvi.
1330.	Pictures from Italy,	Charles Dickens.
1551.	Pictures of Europe,	C. A. Bartol.
1580.	Pierre; Or, The Ambiguities,	Herman Melville.
956.	Pilgrims,	Edward Lytton Bulwer.
1484½.	Pilgrims of the Rhine.	
2249.	Pilgrim's Progress,	John Bunyan.
2173.	Pilgrim Soul, (dialogues),	John P. Schabalie.
2040.	Pillar of Fire,	J. H. Ingraham.

No.	TITLE.	AUTHOR.
1424.	Pilot, The, (Novel),	J. Fennimore Cooper.
34.	Pinkney, William, Life of,	Henry Wheaton.
1425.	Pioneers, (Novel),	J. Fennimore Cooper.
232.	Pitcairn's Island.	
1602.	Plain Talk On Familiar Subjects,	J. G. Holland.
2240.	Plain Words To Young Men,	J. B. Ripley.
1224.	Plant Hunters,	Captain Mayne Reid.
1029.	Played Out,	Annie Thomas.
1033½.	Playing For High Stakes,	Annie Thomas.
1702.	Pleasant Memories,	Mrs. L. H. Signourney.
1788.	Plurality of Worlds,	Edward Hitchcock.
135.	Poets, American,	William C. Bryant.
1544.	Poets and Poetry of the Hebrews,	J. W. Carhart.
1561.	Poets, Bowdoin College,	Edward P. Weston.
110–11.	Poets, British—2 Vols ,	Fitz Green Halleck.
1693.	Poets, British, Beauties of,	George Croly.
1550.	Poets, Gems of,	S. C. Hall.
1543.	Poems, Battle Pieces,	Herman Melville.
1538.	Poems, Charms of Fancy,	Richard Alsop.
1683.	Poems, Fables and Legends,	John G. Saxe.
1689.	Poems, Fifine at the Fair,	Robert Browning.
1673.	Poems, Hidden Life, etc.,	George Macdonald.
1542.	Poems, King Arthur,	Edward Lytton Bulwer.
1591.	Poems, Marble Prophecy, etc.,	J. G. Holland.
1684.	Poems, Pennsylvania Pilgrim, etc.,	John G. Whittier.
1685.	Poems, Tent on the Beach, etc.,	John G. Whittier.
1682.	Poems, Three Books of Song,	Henry W. Longfellow.
1688.	Poems, Zcthar,	B. D. Haskell.
1696.	Poems, Legends and Lyrics,	Adelaide A. Proctor.
1556.	Poems,	William C. Bryant.
1697.	Poems,	Oliver W. Holmes.
1687.	Poems, Home Ballads,	Abbey Allin.
1692.	Poems, (complete),	Edgar A. Poe.
1578.	Poems, Leoni Di Monata, etc.,	James Barron Hope.
1619.	Poems, Mount Vernon, etc.	Harvey Rice.
1573.	Poems, Picture of Women,	George Hill.
1681.	Poems, Songs of the Sierras,	Joaquin Miller.
1610.	Poems, Sunny Hours,	J. W. Carhart.

NO.	TITLE.	AUTHOR.
1581.	Poems, Thirty,	William C. Bryant.
1614.	Poems, War Lyrics, etc.,	Henry H. Brownell.
1676.	Poems, Wayside Flowers,	Carrie Carlton.
1513.	Poetical Quotations,	William Rice.
1501,	Poetical Works, (complete),	Lord Byron.
1694–5.	Poetical Works—2 Vols.,	John G. Whittier.
1568.	Poetical Works,	Walter Scott.
1680.	Poetical Works, etc., of Scott,	F. T Palgrave.
1548.	Poetical Works, (complete),	Martin L. Tupper.
1579.	Poetical Works,	Thomas Hood.
278.	Poetry, and Lectures on,	James Montgomery.
1613.	Poetry, American,	Rufus W. Griswold.
1011.	Point of Honor.	
559.	Polar Sea,	I. I. Hayes.
315.	Polar Sea and Regions,	Professor Leslie, &c.
307.	Polar Sea, Expedition to,	Admiral Wrangell.
1784.	Political Economy,	John Stuart Mill.
266.	Political Economy,	A. Potter.
1750.	Political Economy,	Jean Baptiste Say.
662–3.	Political Writings—2 Vols.,	William Leggett.
585.	Polk, James K., Life of,	James S. Jenkins.
1035.	Poor Humanity,	F. W. Robinson.
300.	Poor Rich Man and Rich Poor Man.	
1737.	Popery, Spirit of.	
2167.	Popery, As It Was and Is,	William Hogan.
1820.	Portraits of My Married Friends,	Uncle Ben.
483.	Potiphar Papers,	George W. Curtiss.
72.	Power of the Soul Over the Body,	George Moore.
961.	Prairie Bird,	Charles A. Murray.
500.	Prairie Traveller,	Captain Marcy.
213.	Praise and Principle.	
1426.	Precaution,	J. Fonnimore Cooper.
2261.	Preciousness of Christ,	J. Thornton.
515.	Pre-Historic Times,	John Lubbock.

PRESCOTT'S WORKS.

400.	Biographical and Critical Miscellanies.	

No.	TITLE.	AUTHOR.
386–8.	Charles The Fifth—3 Vols.	
391–3.	Conquest of Mexico—3 Vols.	
389–90.	Conquest of Peru—2 Vols.	
394–6.	Ferdinand and Isabella—3 Vols.	
397–9.	Philip The Second—3 Vols.	

No.	TITLE.	AUTHOR.
958.	President's Daughter,	Frederika Bremer.
987.	Pride, (Novel).	
2038.	Prince of the House of David,	J. H. Ingraham.
1288.	Prince Eugene and his Times,	Louisa Mühlbach.
1859.	Prison Life and Reflections,	George Thompson.
646.	Prison Life in the South,	A. O. Abbott.
2142.	Private Voice to Public Heart,	Carcline Briggs.
2010.	Problem of Human Destiny,	Orville Dewey.
122–3.	Professions and Trades—2 Vols.,	Edward Hazen.
865.	Profession is not Principle.	
1009.	Professor's Lady,	Berthold Auerbach.
1104.	*Pronouncing Gazetteer of the World,	J. B. Lippincott.
222.	Property and Labor,	Francis Lieber.
480.	Prue and I,	George W. Curtiss.
2210.	Psalms and Hymns.	
1989.	Psalms of David, (chronologically arranged),	F. G. Hibbard.
1063.	Publicans and Sinners,	Miss M. E. Braddon.
1545.	Public and Parlor Readings, (Humorous),	Lewis B. Monroe.
1546.	ditto,	ditto.
1547.	ditto, (Dialogues),	ditto.
1115.	Puck, (Novel),	"Ouida."
904.	Pure Gold from Rivers of Wisdom.	
164–5.	Pursuit of Knowledge—2 Vols.	
35.	Putnam, Israel, Life of,	Oliver W. B. Peabody.
1378.	Put Yourself In His Place,	Charles Reade.
1173.	Quest. (Novel),	
970.	Queen of Denmark,	Mrs. Gore.
1289.	Queen Hortense,	Louisa Mühlbach.
1290.	ditto,	ditto.
1153.	Queen Mab,	Julia Kavanah.
410–16.	Queens of England—7 Vols.,	Agnes Strickland.

NO.	TITLE.	AUTHOR.
623–4.	Queens of France—2 Vols.	Mrs. Forbes Bush.
1644.	Quentin Durward,	Walter Scott.
999.	Quiet Heart,	Mrs. Oliphant.
453–4.	Quitman, John A., Life of—2 Vols.,	J. F. H. Clairbourne.
1016.	Quite Alone,	George A. Sala.
1026.	Race for Wealth,	Mrs. J. H. Riddell.
1889.	Races of Mankind,	Cephas Broadluck.
1013.	Rachel Ray (Novel),	Anthony Trollope.
1028.	Rachel's Secret.	
548.	Rambles in Yucatan,	B. M. Norman.
1496.	Ran Away to Sea,	Captain Mayne Reid.
492.	Raphael; Or, The Pages of the Book of Life at Twenty,	A. De Lamartine.
401–2.	Rationalism in Europe—2 Vols..	W. E. H. Lecky.
992.	Ravenscliffe,	Mrs. Marsh.
1030.	Raymond's Heroine.	

READE'S WORKS.

1368. Cloister and Hearth.
1082½. Foul Play.
1370. Griffith Gaunt.
1372. Love Me Little, Love Me Long.
1373. Never Too Late To Mend.
1374. Never Too Late To Mend.
1375–6. ditto—2 Vols.
1377. Peg Woffington.
1378. Put Yourself In His Place.
1379. White Lies.

NO.	TITLE.	AUTHOR.
1865.	Real Folks,	Mrs. A. D. T. Whitney.
1925.	Recollections of a Policeman,	Thomas Waters.
1782.	Recollections of Past Life,	Henry Holland.
1881.	Records of Five Years,	Grace Greenwood.
2118.	Recreations of a Country Parson.	
1122.	Redburn: His First Voyage,	Herman Melville.
1259.	Red Rover,	J. Fennimore Cooper.
1428.	ditto,	ditto.
1427.	Red Skins,	J. Fennimore Cooper.
1645.	Red Gauntlet,	Walter Scott.
540.	Reed Family, History of,	Jacob W. Reed.
963.	Regent's Daughter,	Charles H. Town.

NO.	TITLE.	AUTHOR.
1169.	Reginald Archer,	Anne M. C. Seemuller,
987.	Reginald Hastings,	Eliot Warburton.
66.	Religion and Fashionable Life,	Alden.
2165.	Religion of Good Sense,	Edward Ricker.
2047.	Religion, Power of on the Mind,	Lindlay Murray.
1836–8.	Religion, Science and Literature—Vols. 1–4–6.	
2016.	Religious Anecdotes—Vol. 1,	Charles Buck.
2007–8.	Religious Magazine—Vols. 3–4.	Ashbel Green.
2239.	Repentance Explained,	Charles Walker.
1552.	Residence On a Georgian Plantation,	Frances Anne Kemble.
1553.	ditto,	ditto.
1129.	Resolution; Or, The Soul of Power,	A. S. Roe.
1826.	Responsibility in Mental Disease,	Henry Maudsley.
903.	Return of Prayers, etc.,	Thomas Goodwin.
59.	Revolt of the Netherlands,	Frederick Schiller.
1739.	Riches Have Wings,	T. S. Arthur.
1595.	Rides and Reveries of Esop Smith,	Martin F. Tupper.
954.	Rienzi,	Edward Lytton Bulwer.
1491.	ditto,	ditto.
1756.	Riley, Captain James, Life and Voyages,	W. W. Riley.
629.	Rise and Decline of Secession,	Parson Brownlow.
2187.	Rise and Progress of Religion in the Soul,	Philip Doddridge.
35.	Rittenhouse, David, Life of,	James Renwick.
2216.	Road to Faith (Jewish Catechism),	Henry Loéb.
1208.	Robinson Crusoe,	Daniel De Foe.
1531.	Robert Falconer,	George Macdonald.
1850-51.	Robertson, F. W., Life and Letters—2 Vols.,	Stafford A. Brooke.
1849.	Robertson, Lectures and Addresses,	F. W. Robertson.
1646.	Rob Roy,	Walter Scott.
1058.	Robin Gray,	Charles Gibbon.
1457.	Roderick Random,	T. Smollett.
976.	Roland Cashel,	Charles Lever.
1400.	Romola,	George Eliot.
1943.	Roman Imperialism,	J. R. Seeley.
1442.	Romance of a Poor Young Man,	Octave Feuillet.
1165.	Romance of the Republic,	L. Maria Child.
26.	Rosamond, and Other Stories,	Maria Edgeworth.

NO.	TITLE.	AUTHOR.
780.	Roscerans' Campaigns with 14th Army Corps.	
961.	Rose D'Albret,	G. P. R. James.
1805.	Rose Douglass,	S. R. W.
1004.	Rose of Ashurst,	Mrs. Marsh.
1396.	Rose Mather,	Mrs. Mary J. Holmes.
1515.	Roughing It,	Mark Twain.
1341.	Round-About Papers and Lectures,	W. M. Thackeray.
970.	Royal Favorite,	Mrs. Gore.
149–50.	Ruins of Ancient Cities—2 Vols.,	Charles Bucke.
860.	Rules for Men-of-War,	U. P. Levy, U. S. Navy.
1789.	Rural Studies, etc.	
977.	Russell (Novel),	G. P. R. James.
1181.	Ruth (Novel).	
964.	Safia (Novel),	Roger De Beauvoir.
1225.	Sailor Boy,	Oliver Optic.
747.	Sailors' Magazine.	
499.	Sailing on the Nile,	Laurent Laporte.
790.	Saints' Rest,	Richard Baxter.
1668.	Salmagundi,	Washington Irving.
22.	Sallust, Works of,	R. J. S. Watson.
90–91.	Samuel Johnson, Life and Writings—2 Vols.,	William Page.
206.	Sanford and Merton,	Thomas Day.
1023,	Sans Merci,	George Lawrence.
1775.	Saratoga in 1901,	Eli Perkins.
564–5.	Santa Fé Expedition—2 Vols.,	George W. Kendall.
1429.	Satanstoe.	J. Fennimore Cooper.
1140–41.	Say and Seal—2 Vols.	
762.	Sayings and Doings of Sam. Slick.	
798.	Scenes and Songs of Social Life,	Isaac F. Shepard.
67	Scenes Where the Tempter has Triumphed.	
1771.	School and Army.	

SCHOOL BOOKS.

824,	Algebra, Elementary,	Charles Davies.
840.	Arithmetic, Intellectual,	Joseph Ray.
841	ditto,	ditto.
845.	Arithmetic, Practical.	Joseph Ray.

NO.	TITLE.	AUTHOR.
844.	Arithmetic,	James B. Thompson.
826.	Arithmetic,	Daniel Adams.
827.	Arithmetic,	Charles Davies.
828.	ditto,	ditto
825.	Arithmetic, University,	Charles Davies.
687.	Geography,	S. Augustus Mitchell.
806.	Geometry and Trigonometry,	Benjamin Greenleaf.
688.	ditto,	ditto.
832.	Grammar, English (First Series),	Peter Bullion.
821.	Grammar, English,	Peter Bullion.
822.	ditto,	ditto.
823.	Grammar, English,	Thomas W. Harvey.
835.	Latin Grammar,	Peter Bullion.
833.	Latin Grammar,	Andrrews & Stoddard.
834.	Latin Reader,	Andrews & Stoddard.
836.	Latin Reader,	Peter Bullion.
837.	Latin Reader (Livy),	J. L. Lincoln.
842.	Reader, Second Eclectic,	William H. McGuffey.
843.	ditto,	ditto.
818.	Reader, Fourth Eclectic,	William H. McGuffey.
817.	Reader, Fifth Eclectic,	William H. McGuffey.
818½.	Reader, American First Class Book.	
805.	Reader, English.	
819.	Reader, Third National,	Parker & Watson.
820.	ditto,	ditto.
809.	Reader, Fourth,	Parker & Watson.
810.	ditto,	ditto.
807.	Reader, Fifth,	Parker & Watson.
808.	ditto,	ditto.
811.	Reader, National Preceptor,	J. Olney.
814.	Reader, Fourth New School,	Charles W. Sanders.
815.	ditto,	ditto.
816.	Reader, Fifth,	G. S. Hillard.
812	Reader, Young Ladies',	Anna N. Russell.
813.	Reader, Young Ladies',	Charles Saunders.
838.	Speller, Elementary,	Parker & Watson.
839.	ditto,	ditto.
829.	Speller, National,	Parker & Watson.

NO.	TITLE.	AUTHOR.
297.	Science and Literature,	Lord Brougham, etc.
1812.	Science for Leisure Hours,	Richard A. Proctor.
301.	Science, Martyrs of,	David Brewster.
1940.	Science of Nature *vs.* Man,	Noah Porter.
1809.	Science, Philosophy and Morals,	Herbert Spencer.
75.	Science, Wonders of,	Henry Mayhew.
613–14.	Scott, General, Life of—2 Vols.,	Autobiography.

SCOTT'S WORKS.

1630. Anne of Geirstein.
1631. Antiquary.
1632. Bethrothed Highland Widow.
1633. Bride of Lammermore.
1648. Castle Dangerous.
1634. Count Robert of Paris.
1635. Fair Maid of Perth.
1636. Fortunes of Nigel.
1637. Guy Mannering.
1638. Heart of Mid-Lothian.
1639. Ivanhoe.
1640. Kenilworth.
1641. Legend of Montrose.
1642. Old Mortality.
1643. Peveril of the Peak.
1644. Quentin Durward.
1645. Red Gauntlet.
1646. Rob Roy.
1647. St. Ronan's Well.
1648. Surgeon's Daughter.
1649. Talisman.
1650. The Monastery.
1651. The Abbot.
1652. The Pirate.
1653. Waverley.
1654. Woodstock.

NO.	TITLE.	AUTHOR.
1908.	Scottish Life and Character,	E. B. Ramsey.
1751.	Scrambles Among the Alps,	Edward Whymper.
2220.	Scripture Biography,	T. H. Gallandet.
2050.	Scripture Cabinet,	Erwin House.
713.	Scribner's Monthly (1871)—Vol. 2.	
1430.	Sea Lions,	J. Fennimore Cooper.
2120.	Seaboard Parish,	George Macdonald.
264.	Seaward's Shipwreck,	Jane Potter.
1807.	Secret Service, U. S.,	George P. Burnham.
966.	Self (Novel),	
979.	Self Control,	Mary Brunton.

NO.	TITLE.	AUTHOR.
1905.	Self Culture, etc.,	O. S. Fowler.
955.	Self Devotion,	Miss Campbell.
2229.	Select Remains,	John Mason.
1883.	Select Tales,	Hannah More.
2259.	Self Knowledge,	John Mason.
1992.	Semi-Centennial Celebration, Andover, Massachusetts.	
1171.	Septimus Felton,	Nathaniel Hawthorne.
2059.	Sermons from the Pulpit,	H. B. Bascom.
2017.	Sermons, etc.,	Ralph Erskine.
2155.	Sermons,	W. Hunter.
2197.	Sermons—Vol. 1,	D. D. Davisson.
2000.	Sermons,	Henry Melville.
2134.	Sermons.	C. H. Spurgeon.
1780.	Sermons, Addresses, etc ,	Thomas H. Huxley.
2009.	Sermons and African Repository.	
2029.	Sermons for the People,	F. D. Huntington.
2024.	Sermons, Lectures and Speeches,	Cardinal Wiseman.
2122.	Sermons: Nature and Life,	Robert Collyer.
2234.	Sermons on Intemperance,	Lyman Beecher.
1990.	Sermons, Plymouth Church (1st Series),	H. W. Beecher.
2002-3.	Sermons, Plymouth Church—2 Vols,	H. W. Beecher.
2080.	Sermons, Reviews and Essays,	James Floy.
794-96.	Seward, Sir Edward, Shipwreck of—3 Vols.,	Miss Jane Porter.
797.	Shabby-Genteel,	William M. Thackeray.
1945.	ditto,	ditto.
1584.	Shakers and Shakerism,	F. W. Evans.
1517.	Shakespeare—Vol 2.	
1691.	Shakespeare (Complete),	Charles Knight.
1521-28.	Shakespeare's Works—8 Vols.,	World Edition.
2203.	Shepard, Thomas, Life of,	John A. Albro.
984.	Shirley,	Currer Bell.
1806.	Short Stories.	
984.	Sidonia the Sorceress,	William Meinhold.
641.	Signers of Declaration of Independence,	Charles A. Goodrich.
1401.	Silas Marner and Clerical Life,	George Eliot.
2146.	Silent Partner,	Elizabeth S. Phelps.
977.	Simple Story,	Mrs. Inchbald.
2030.	Sin and Redemption,	D. N. Sheldon.

NO.	TITLE.	AUTHOR.
988.	Singleton Fontenoy,	James Hannay.
1027.	Sir Brook Fossbroke,	Charles Lever.
985.	Sir Edward Graham,	Catharine Sinclair.
1047.	Sir Harry Hotspur,	Anthony Trollope.
999.	Sir Jasper Carew,	Charles Lever.
1913.	Sir Roger De Coverley,	Spectator.
979.	Sir Theodore Broughton,	G. P. R. James.
1690.	Sister Margaret,	Mrs. C. M. Edwards.
1216.	Six of One, and Half-a-Dozen of the Other,	E. E. Hale, etc.
1670.	Sketch Book,	Washington Irving.
1707.	Sketches,	Mrs. Sigourney.
2252.	Sketches and Incidents,	George Peck.
1331.	Sketches by Boz,	Charles Dickens.
1931.	Skirmishes and Sketches,	Gail Hamilton.
1840.	Slave Life in Rome (Tale).	
659.	Smith, Captain John,	George C. Hill.
30.	Smith, Captain John,	George S. Hillard.
1500.	Smollet's Works (Complete),	Tobias Smollet.
966.	Smuggler,	G. P. R. James.
1366.	Snarleyow,	Captain Marryatt.
2056.	Sober Thoughts on Staple Themes,	Richard Randolph.
1786.	Social Welfare and Human Progress,	C. S. Henry.
1884.	Soil Culture,	J. H. Walden.
660.	Soldier Boy,	William T. Adams.
1880.	Soldiers, Illustrious, Sketches of,	James G. Wilson.
2181.	Soldiers of the Bible,	W. M. Thayer.
269.	Son of a Genius,	Mrs. Hofland.
2225.	Songs of Zion.	
15.	Sophocles' Tragedies,	Oxford Translation.
1858.	Sorgho and Imphee,	Henry S. Olcott
422.	Sound, On,	John Tyndall.
378.	Source of the Nile,	Captain Speke.
462.	South Africa,	Bayard Taylor.
1705.	South in Secession Times,	Edmund Kirk.
1042.	So Runs the World Away,	Mrs. A. C. Steele.
1029.	Sowing the Wind,	E. Lynn Linton.
432–35.	Spanish Conquest in America—4 Vols.,	Arthur Help.
1669.	Spanish Papers,	Washington Irving.

NO.	TITLE.	AUTHOR.
155–6.	Spectator (Selections)—2 Vols.,	Addison, Steele, etc.
1507.	Speeches at the Bar,	John P. Curran.
1760.	Spiritual Manifestations,	Robert Hare.
1988.	Spiritual Gleanings.	
2245.	Spoiled Child,	William C. Brownlee.
1431.	Spy, The,	J. Fennimore Cooper.
1407.	Star and Cloud,	A. S. Roe.
1843.	Star Papers,	Henry W. Beecher.
29.	Stark, John, Life of,	Edward Everett.
1844.	Steamboat and Railroad,	S. A. Howland.
652	Stewart's Adventures in Capturing Murrell, etc.,	H. R Howard.
1156.	St. Elmo,	Augusta J. Evans.
971.	Step-Mother,	G. P. R. James.
1042.	Stern Necessity,	F. W. Robinson.
737.	Stock Exchange,	John Francis.
609.	Stonewall Jackson,	A Virginian.
1499.	Story's Miscellaneous Writings,	Joseph Story.
1703.	Story of a Bad Boy,	Thomas B. Aldrich.
1727.	Story of the Civil War.	
1127.	Story of a Millionaire,	Louisa Mühlbach.
1300.	Story of Sibylle,	Octave Feuillet.
610.	Story of the Great March,	G. W. Nichols.
1342.	Stories. Ballads, etc.,	William M. Thackeray.
275.	Stories for Young Persons.	
2162.	Stories from the Moorland,	Miss Lizzie Bates.
78.	Stories of the Island World,	Charles Nordhoff.
1057.	Strange Adventures of a Pheaton,	William Black.
1492.	Strange Story,	Edward Lytton Bulwer.
1061.	Strangers and Pilgrims,	Miss M. E. Braddon.
1647.	St. Ronan's Well,	Walter Scott.
958.	Strife and Peace; Or, Scenes in Norway,	Frederika Bremer.
990.	Stuart of Dunleath,	Caroline Norton.
37.	Steuben, Baron, Life of,	Francis Bowen.
757.	Student and Schoolmate (1860).	
758.	ditto, (ditto.)	
1831.	Study of Sociology,	Herbert Spencer.
1011.	St. Olaves.	

NO.	TITLE.	AUTHOR.
379.	Suburban Home Grounds,	F. J. Scott.
1566.	Suburban Sketches,	W. D. Howells.
1912.	Success and Its Conditions,	Edwin P. Whipple.
1721.	Successful Merchant,	William Arthur.
250.	Suffer and be Strong,	E. Jane Cate.
1588.	Sufferings, etc., of Unionists During the Rebellion,	A. O. W.
1648	Surgeon's Daughter, etc.,	Walter Scott.
1206.	Swell Life at Sea.	
92–95.	Swiss Family Robinson—4 Vols.	
1447.	ditto.	
2159.	Sword and Garment,	L. T. Townsend.
1006.	Sword and Gown,	George Lawrence.
1624.	Sybil (Novel),	B. Disraeli.
1199.	Sydnie Adrience; Or, Trying the World,	Amanda M. Douglass.
1010.	Sylvia's Lovers,	Mrs. Gaskell.
2199.	Systematic Beneficience,	Abel Stephens.
1803.	Table D'Hote and Drawing-Room.	
1857.	Table-Talk,	Samuel Rogers.
20–21.	Tacitus—2 Vols.,	Oxford Translation.
779.	Tale of the Alamo,	Augusta J. Evans.
1332.	Tale of Two Cities,	Charles Dickens.
1474.	ditto,	ditto.
850–53.	Tales of The Castle—4 Vols.,	La Comtesse De Genlis.
2224.	Tales for the People,	Miss Sedgwick.
963.	Tales from the German.	Translated by Oxenford-Feiling.
1671.	Tales of a Traveler,	Washington Irving.
1179.	Tales of Woman's Trials,	Mrs. S. C. Hall.
1198.	ditto,	ditto.
1445.	Tales, Romances and Extravaganzas,	Thomas Hood.
1649.	Talisman,	Walter Scott.
1739.	Tall Oaks from Little Acorns,	William A. Alcott.
1627.	Tancred (Novel),	B. Disraeli.
1947.	Tanner-Boy (U. S. Grant),	Major Penniman.
2081.	Taylor, E. T., Rev. (Sailor Preacher),	Haven-Russel.
669.	Taylor, General, Life of.	
1810.	Teacher and Parent,	Charles Northend.
895.	Tell-Tale, or Home Secrets,	Mrs. E. Stuart Phelps.

NO.	TITLE.	AUTHOR.
1397.	Tempest and Sunshine,	Mrs. M. J. Holmes.
2198.	Temperance Lectures,	Eliphalet Nott.
1598.	Temperance Speeches, Poems, etc.,	Charles Jewett.
1887.	Temperance Text Books,	F. R Lees.
1599.	Temperance Tracts,	Tract Society.
887–90.	Temperance Tales—Vols. 3–4–5–6.	Lucius M. Sargent.
1033.	Tenants of Malory,	J. L. Le Fanu.
1622.	Ten Thousand Wonderful Things,	Edmond F. King.
1585.	Ten Years Among the Mail Bags.	
24.	Terrence's Comedies,	Henry T. Paley.

THACKERAY'S WORKS.

1334. Adventures of Philip.
1335. Book of Snobs and Sketches.
1380. ditto.
1336. Christmas Book.
1337. Esmond and Barry Lyndon.
1338. History of Pendennis.
1381. ditto.
1339. Hoggarty Diamond.
1340. Paris, Irish and Eastern Sketch-Book.
1382. ditto, ditto.
1341. Round-About Papers and Lectures.
1342. Stories, Ballads, etc.
1343. The Newcomes.
1383. ditto.
1344. The Virginians.
1384. ditto.
1345. Vanity Fair.

NO.	TITLE.	AUTHOR.
1265.	Thackeray, Miss, Works (Complete),	Anne I. Thackeray.
1038.	That Boy of Norcott's,	Charles Lever.
1651.	The Abbot,	Walter Scott.
1026.	The Beauclercs,	Charles Clarke.
1142.	The Blemmertons,	J. J. Nicholson.
2065.	The Book and Its Story,	L. N. R.
1706.	The Boy That Had His Own Way,	Walter Aimwell.
1037.	The Bramleighs,	Charles Lever.
1720.	The Caravan,	Wilhelm Hauff.
312.	The Cousins.	
1432.	The Crater; Or, Vulcan's Peak,	J. Fennimore Cooper.
954.	The Czarina,	Mrs. Hofland.
1712.	The Doctor, etc.	

NO.	TITLE.	AUTHOR.
1036.	The Dower House,	Annie Thomas.
228.	The Earth,	W. M. Higgins.
731.	The Educator,	John M. Spear.
970.	The Elves (Novel),	L. Tieck.
2169.	The End of the World,	John Cumming.
1226.	The Escaped Nun.	
991.	The Fate (Novel),	G. P. R. James.
2189.	The Forge and Pulpit.	
982.	The Forgery (Novel),	G. P. R. James.
2214.	The Giants, and How to Fight Them,	Richard Newton.
2253.	The Great Supper,	Ezra D. Kinney.
2202.	The Great Teacher,	John Harris.
2112.	The Heart: Its Tendency to Evil,	D. G. Gozder.
1864.	The Hearth-Stone,	Samuel Osgood.
957.	The Home (Novel),	Frederika Bremer.
1925.	The Island Home,	Christopher Romaunt.
960.	The Jew (Novel),	Spindler.
962.	The Jilt (Novel).	
1117.	The Lamplighter.	
1711.	The Little Spaniard.	Mary Mannering.
785.	The Lofty and Lowly.	
1819.	The Moon.	R. A. Proctor.
1798.	The Moon, Wonders of.	Amedee Guillemin.
1343.	The Newcomes,	William M. Thackeray.
1383.	ditto,	ditto.
1928.	The News Boys.	
984.	The Ogilvies,	Miss Muloch.
468.	The Old Regime and The Revolution,	Alexis De Tocqueville.
2044	The Other Life,	William H. Holcombe.
1652.	The Pirate,	Walter Scott.
1367.	The Poacher,	Capt. Marryatt.
1532.	The Portent (Story),	George Macdonald.
1433.	The Prairie (Novel),	J. Fennimore Cooper.
1201.	The Professor,	Currer Bell.
861–63.	The Rambler—Vols. 1–2–4.	Samuel Johnson.
2109.	The Redeemer,	Edmond Pressensé.
1291.	The Right One,	Maria S. Schwartz.
1219.	The Rose Garden.	

NO.	TITLE.	AUTHOR.
1250.	The Snow Man,	George Lord.
2076.	The Stars and the Angels.	
490.	The Stone Mason,	A. De Lamartine.
1344.	The Virginians,	William M. Thackeray.
1384.	ditto,	ditto.
1046.	The Warden,	Anthony Trollope.
985.	The Wilmingtons,	Mrs. Marsh.
792.	The Young Cadet,	Mrs. Hofland.
1625.	The Young Duke,	B. Disraeli.
1018.	Theodore Leigh,	Annie Thomas.
658.	Theological Subjects,	William S. Andrews.

THIERS' WORKS.

357–61. Consulate and Empire—5 Volumes.

353-56. French Revolution—4 Volumes.

NO.	TITLE.	AUTHOR.
765.	Things I Saw Abroad.	
1790.	Thirty Years in the Harem,	Autobiography.
981.	Thirty Years Since,	G. P. R. James.
1612.	Thorburn, Grant, Life of,	Autobiography.
2043.	Thought Hives,	Theodore L. Cuyler.
981.	Three Sisters (Novel),	G. H. Lewes.
374.	Three Visits to Madagascar,	William Ellis.
112–13.	Three Voyages—2 Vols.,	W. E. Parry.
1260.	Tricotrin (Novel),	"Ouida."
2039.	Throne of David,	J. H. Ingraham.
9.	Thucydides,	H. Dale.
999.	Ticonderoga (Novel),	G. P. R. James.
989.	Time the Avenger,	Mrs. Marsh.
1022.	Toilers of the Sea,	Victor Hugo.
1616.	Tom Brown at Oxford (Part 1),	Thomas Hughes.
1617.	Tom Brown at Oxford (Part 2),	ditto.
1618.	Tom Brown at Rugby,	Thomas Hughes.
1459.	Tom Jones, History of.	Henry Fielding.
1252.	Tom Pippin's Wedding.	
801.	Toothache, and Other Stories.	
1057.	To the Bitter End,	M. E. Braddon.
1060.	Too Soon (Novel),	Katherine S. Macquoid.

NO.	TITLE.	AUTHOR
1301.	Too Strange, Not to be True,	Georgianna Fullerton.
2226.	Torn Bible,	Alice Somerton.
2042.	Tract Series,	Tract Society.
461.	Travels in Arabia,	Bayard Taylor.
484.	Travels in Armenia,	Robert Curzon.
530.	Travels in Central Asia,	Arminius Vámbéry.
664.	Travels in England, France, etc.,	George F. Haskins.
591.	Travels in Europe, etc.,—Vol. 1,	Prime.
1768.	Travels in Europe—Vol. 2,	George Catlin.
653–4.	Travels in Greece, Turkey, etc.,—2 Vols.	
377.	Travels in South Africa,	David Livingstone.
635.	ditto,	ditto.
516–17.	Travels in Yucatan—2 Vols.,	John L. Stevens.
311.	Travels of Marco Polo,	Hugh Murray.
209.	Travels of Mungo Park.	
217.	Trees of America,	Uncle Philip.
1231.	Tricotrin (Novel),	"Ouida."
2006.	Trinitarian System,	David Harrower.
2075.	Trinitarian Theology,	James Forrest.
961.	Triumphs of Time,	Mrs. Marsh.
1149.	True as Steel,	Marion Harland.
1044.	True to Herself,	F. W. Robinson.
1168.	True to the Last,	A. S. Roe.
1116.	Trumps (Romance),	George W. Curtiss
992.	Tutor's Ward.	
439.	Twenty Years in the Phillipine Islands,	Paul P. Gironiere.
238.	Twin Brother.	
1623.	Twice Told Tales—Vol. 2,	Nathaniel Hawthorne.
1434.	Two Admirals,	J Fennimore Cooper.
1192.	Two Guardians.	
1498.	Two Life Paths,	Louisa Mühlbach.
2022.	Two Pictures,	M. J. McIntosh.
1061.	Two Widows,	Annie Thomas.
285.	Two Years Before the Mast,	R. H. Dana.

TYNDALL'S WORKS.

426.	Forms of Water.	424.	Lectures in America.
421.	Fragments of Science.	425.	Light and Electricity.

NO.	TITLE.	AUTHOR.
419.	Heat as a Mode of Motion. 423.	Michael Faraday.
420.	Hours of Exercise in the Alps.	
	422.	On Sound.

NO.	TITLE.	AUTHOR.
486.	Typee; Or, Four Months in the Marquesas,	Herman Melville.
1232.	Una and Her Paupers.	
1248.	Unawares (Novel).	
501-2.	Uncivilized Races of Men—2 Vols.,	J. G. Wood.
1185.	Unclaimed: A Story of English Life,	An English Woman.
1674.	Uncle Sam's Palace,	Emma Wellmont.
1017.	Uncle Silas,	J. S. Le Fanu.
1333.	Uncommercial Traveller,	Charles Dickens.
1178.	Under the Cedars (Novel),	Alice J. Hatch.
1774.	Under the Trees (Miscellaneous Papers),	Samuel I. Prime.
1041.	Under Foot (Novel),	Alton Clyde
1454.	Under Two Flags (Novel),	"Ouida."
2084.	Unitarianism Defined,	Frederick A. Farley.
2111.	Universalism, Guide to,	Thomas Whittemore.
1946.	Universal Gazetteer (1832).	
1539.	Universal Progress,	Herbert Spencer.
2171.	Universal Salvation, Debate on,	E. M. Pingree-N. L. Rice.
726.	United States Magazine, Volume 1 —1864.	
727.	" " " 2 —1864.	
728.	" " " 3 —1865.	
729.	" " " 4 —1865.	
730.	" " " 5 —1866.	
959.	Unloved One,	Mrs. Hofland.
647.	Up and Down and Around the World,	James Brooks.
1794.	Useful Arts—2 Vols.,	Jacob Bigelow.
2096.	Vale of Cedars; Or, The Martyr,	Grace Aguilar.
32.	Vane, Sir Henry, Life of,	Charles W. Upham.
1345.	Vanity Fair,	William M. Thackeray.
1136.	Vandermarck Richard,	Mrs. S. S. Harris.
1137.	ditto,	ditto.
1261.	Vashti; Or, Until Death Us Do Part,	Augusta J. Evans.
224.	Vegetable Food of Man.	
1626.	Venetia (Novel),	B. Disraeli.
153-4.	Venetian History—2 Vols.	

NO.	TITLE.	AUTHOR.
1757.	Verdant Green's Adventures,	Cuthbert Bede.
965.	Veronica (Novel),	Zchokke.
1044.	ditto,	ditto.
2174.	Vestry Harp (Hymn-Book),	N. M. Perkins.
214.	Vicar of Wakefield,	Oliver Goldsmith.
1986.	ditto,	ditto.
2222	Vicars, Capt. Headley.	
2223.	ditto.	
896.	View of Christ,	Caleb Kimball.
1138.	Villette (Novel),	Currer Bell.
997.	ditto,	ditto.
1835.	Village Life in New England (Novel),	H. W. Beecher.
1028.	Village On the Cliff,	Miss Thackeray.
18.	Virgil, Works of,	Theodore A. Buckley.
341.	Virginia Illustrated (Adventure),	Porte Crayon, etc.
666.	Visit to the United States (1841),	Joseph Sturge.
1628.	Vivian Grey (Novel),	B. Disraeli.
1045.	Vivian Romance,	Mortimer Collins.
2113.	Voices of the Soul Answered in God,	John Reid.
1534.	Voltaire,	John Morley.
1902.	Voters' Text Book, Record of Rebellion, etc.,	James M. Hiatt.
272.	Voyages Round the World.	
409.	Voyage Round the World,	Charles Darwin.
2098.	Voyage to the Celestial Country,	G. B. Cheever.
1562	Walfried (Novel),	Berthold Auerbach.
534.	Walter Scott, Life of,	George Allan.
1021.	Walter Goring (Novel),	Annie Thomas.
1718.	Walter's Tour in the East,	Daniel E. Eddy.
2212.	Walk About Zion,	John A. Clark.
1180.	War Path (Adventure),	J. B. Jones.
38.	Warren, Joseph, Life of,	Alexander H. Everett.
497.	Washington Irving,	Charles Adams.
674.	Washington, Life of.	
166-7.	Washington, Life of—2 Vols.,	James K. Paulding.
1033.	Waterdale Neighbors.	
1435.	Water-Witch,	J. Fennimore Cooper.
2257.	Watts, On the Mind.	
1436.	Ways of the Hour,	J. Fennimore Cooper.

NO.	TITLE.	AUTHOR.
32.	Wayne, Anthony, Life of,	John Armstrong.
2254.	Way of Holiness,	Mrs. Phœbe Palmer.
2143.	Way of Life,	Charles Hodge.
2132.	Way of Life,	Thomas Guthrie.
2248.	Waymarks of the Pilgrimage,	G. B. Cheever.
1123.	Way of the World,	William T. Adams.
978.	Wayside Cross (Novel),	E. H. Milman.
309.	Wealth and Worth.	
1762.	Wealth of Nations,	Adam Smith.
1114.	Web and Woof of Life,	William G. Cambridge.
2048.	Wesley, John, Life of,	Richard Watson.
1438.	Wept of Wish-ton-Wish,	J. Fennimore Cooper.
1709.	Whaling and Fishing,	Charles Nordhoff.
118–19.	Whale Fishery—2 Vols.,	Uncle Philip.
1909.	What Answer?	Anna Dickinson.
1935.	ditto,	ditto.
85.	What's to be Done?	
1906.	What to Do and Why,	Nelson Sizer.
1493–4.	What Will He Do With It?—2 Vols.,	E. Lytton Bulwer.
1015.	ditto,	ditto.
1045.	Which is the Heroine?	
968.	White Boy (Novel),	Mrs. S. C. Hall
1195.	White-Jacket; Or, The World in a Man-of-War,	Herman Melville.
1379.	White Lies (Novel),	George Reade.
967.	White Slave (Novel).	
205.	Who Shall be Greatest?	Mary Howitt.
1014.	Wife's Evidence,	W. G. Wills.
990.	Wife's Sister,	Mrs. Hulback.
1148.	Wilfred Cumbermede,	George Macdonald.
466.	Wild Men and Wild Beasts,	Gordon Cumming.
1894.	Wild Sports in the Far West,	Frederick Gerstæcker.
1817.	Wilkes, Sheridan, Fox,	W. F. Rae.
30.	Wilson, Alexander, Life of,	William B. O. Peabody.
1569.	Windfalls,	
1437.	Wing and Wing,	J. Fennimore Cooper.
1728.	Winifred Bertram.	
555.	Wisconsin Historical Collections (1857).	

NO.	TITLE.	AUTHOR.
542.	Wisconsin in War of the Rebellion,	Love.
543.	ditto,	ditto.
544.	Wisconsin Military History,	E. B. Quiner.
1874.	Wit and Wisdom of Don Quixote.	
1120.	Wolfsden,	J. B.
1672.	Wolfret's Roost,	Washington Irving.
271.	Woman an Enigma.	
226.	Woman in America,	Mrs. A. J. Graves.
1057.	Woman's Vengeance,	James Payn.
556.	Women's Work in the Civil War,	L. P. Brackett.
1130.	Women Our Angel,	A. S. Roe.
2094-5.	Women of Israel—Vols. 1-2,	Grace Aguilar.
1929.	Women's Rights and Spiritualism,	Fred Felio.
976.	Women's Trials, Tales of,	Mrs. S. C. Hall.
1799.	Wonders of Vegetation,	Fulgence Marion.
1800.	Wonders of Water,	Gaston Tissandier.
464.	Wonders of the Yellowstone,	James Richardson.
1049.	Won, Not Wooed,	James Payn.
983.	Woodman (Novel),	G. P. R. James.
1654.	Woodstock,	Walter Scott.
1932.	Wool Gathering,	Gail Hamilton.
2164.	Words in Season,	Henry B. Browning,
642.	World as It Is,	Samuel Perkins.
1825.	Work and Play,	Horace Bushnell.
1770.	Work and Wages,	Thomas Brassey.
776.	Workingman's Companion.	
1461.	Works of Fielding ("Amelia"),	Henry Fielding.
2188.	Works of Puritan Divines,	John Howe.
1039.	Wrecked in Port,	Edmund Yates.
1439.	Wyandott (Novel),	J. Fennimore Cooper.
778.	Wylder's Hand,	J. S. Le Fanu.
965.	Wyoming (Novel),	George Peck.
448.	ditto,	ditto.
1700.	Yankee in Canada, Anti-Slavery Papers, etc.,	Henry D. Thoreau.
1251.	Yankee Middy.	Oliver Optic
1677.	Yankee Prisoner Loose in Dixie,	J. J. Geer.
2064.	Yesterday, To-Day and Forever,	Edward H. Bickersteth.

NO.	TITLE.	AUTHOR.
1713.	Young America in Germany,	Oliver Optic.
1255.	Young America in Norway and Sweden,	Oliver Optic.
2100.	Young Christian,	Jacob Abbott.
2130.	ditto,	ditto.
253.	Young Crusoe,	Mrs. Hofland.
1000.	Young Husband,	Mrs. Grey.
1564–5.	Young Knighthood—2 Vols.,	E. Foxton.
1244.	Young Lieutenant,	Oliver Optic.
1942.	Young Man's Friend,	John A. James.
1730.	Young Man's Guide,	William A. Alcott.
1888.	Young Men, Lectures to,	Rufus W. Clark.
2123.	Young Men, Lectures to,	Henry W. Beecher.
2151.	ditto,	ditto.
2232.	Young Men of the Bible,	Joseph A. Collins.
267.	Young Sailor,	Mrs M. S Dana
1860.	Yousef: A Crusade in the East,	J. Ross Browne.
986.	Zanoni (Novel),	Edward Lytton Bulwer.
1495.	ditto,	ditto.
965.	Zoe (Novel),	Geraldine E. Jewsbury.
594.	Zouave Reminiscences.	

GERMAN BOOKS.

NO.	TITLE.				AUTHOR
1500-0.	Familien Blätter (1874).				
1957.	Franco-German War (1870-'71),				John S. C. Abbott.
1500-(1).	German-Franco War	1870-71,	Part	1-2,	Grand Gen'l Staff.
1500-(2).	"	"	"	3-4,	"
1500-(3).	"	"	"	5,	"
1500-(4).	"	"	"	6,	"
1500-(5).	"	"	"		"
1500-(6).	"	"	"		"
1500-(7).	"	"	"		"
1500-(8).	"	"	"		"

GOETHE'S COMPLETE WORKS.

1966.	Volumes	1-2.
1967.	"	3-4.
1968.	"	5-6.
1969.	"	7-8.
1970.	"	9-10.
1971.	"	11-12.
1972.	"	13-14.
1973.	"	15-16.
1974.	"	17-18.
1975.	"	19-20.
1976.	"	21-22.
1977.	"	23-24.
1978.	"	25-26.
1979.	"	27-28.
1980.	"	29-30.
1981.	"	31-32.

NO.	TITLE.		AUTHOR.
1982.	Volumes	33–34.	
1983.	"	35–36.	

1958.	Life of Abraham Lincoln,	Frank Crosby.
1959.	Novels,	Henry Zschokke.
1960.	Novels,	ditto.
1961.	Novels,	ditto.
1984.	Pilgrim's Progress,	John Bunyan.

SCHILLER'S COMPLETE WORKS.

1962.	Volumes	1–3.
1963.	"	4–6.
1964.	"	7–9.
1965.	"	10–12.

1954. Winterfield's History of Franco-German War of 1870–'71.

1955–6. William I., King of Prussia—2 Vols., A. H. Brandrupp.

1985. John Nelson's Day-Book (Swedish).

HARPER'S SELECT NOVELS.

NO.	TITLE.	AUTHOR.
958.	A Diary,	Frederika Bremer.
1056.	A Girl's Romance,	F. W. Robinson.
1046.	A Siren.	T. Adolphus Trollope.
980.	A Whim,	G. P. R. James.
1009.	Abel Drake's Wife,	John Saunders.
956.	Adam Brown,	H. Smith.
988.	Adelaide Lindsay,	Mrs. Marsh.
997.	Agnes Sorell,	G. P. R. James.
997.	Agatha's Husband,	Miss Mulock.
963.	Agincourt,	G. P. R. James.
1021.	Agnes,	Mrs. Oliphant.
991.	Aims and Obstacles,	G. P. R. James.
978.	Alamance.	
1054.	Albert Lunel,	Lord Brougham.
1031.	Alec Forbes,	George Macdonald.
955.	Alice,	Edward Lytton Bulwer.
1025	All In the Dark,	J. S. Le Fanu.
968.	Amaury,	Alexander Dumas.
972.	Amelia Wyndham,	Mrs. Marsh.
961.	Amy Herbert,	Miss Sewell.
995.	Anna Hammer,	Temme.
1050.	Anne Furness.	
1014.	Annis Warleigh's Fortunes,	Holme Lee.
1049.	Anteros,	George Lawrence.
986.	Antonina,	Wilkie Collins.
959.	Arabella Stuart,	G. P. R. James.
962.	Arrah Neil,	G. P. R. James.
963.	Arthur Arundel,	H. Smith.

NO.	TITLE.	AUTHOR.
991.	Arthur Conway,	E. H. Milman.
960.	Arthur,	Eugene Sue.
969.	Ascanio,	Dumas.
1005.	Athelings,	Margaret Oliphant.
999.	Aubrey,	Mrs. Marsh.
1010.	Aurora Floyd,	Miss M. E. Braddon.
968.	Author's Daughter,	Mary Howitt.
1001.	Avillion,	Miss Mulock.
1042.	Baffled,	Julius Goddard.
958.	Banker's Wife,	Mrs. Gore.
1014.	Barbara's History,	Amelia B. Edwards.
1040.	Barchester Powers,	Anthony Trollope.
1010.	Barrington,	Charles Lever.
975.	Beauchamp,	G. P. R. James.
1040.	Beggar On Horseback,	James Payn.
1021.	Belton Estate,	Anthony Trollope.
1019.	Belial.	
1042.	Beneath the Wheels.	
1028.	Bernthal,	Louisa Mühlbach.
958.	Birthright,	Mrs. Gore.
1029.	Black Sheep,	Edmund Yates.
1063.	Blue Ribbon.	
967.	Bosom Friend,	Mrs. Grey.
1025.	Bound to the Wheel,	John Saunders.
1035.	Brakespeare,	George Lawrence.
966	Breach of Promise.	
1048.	Bred in the Bone,	James Payn.
1053.	Bridge of Glass,	F. W. Robinson.
1033½.	Brother's Bet,	Emilie Flygare Carlen.
980.	Brothers and Sisters,	Frederika Bremer.
1008.	Brown and Jones,	Anthony Trollope.
1034.	Brownlows,	Mrs. Oliphant.
973.	Bush Rangers,	Charles Rowcroft.
1031.	Called To Account,	Miss Annie Thomas.
1033.	Carlyon's Year,	James Payn.
1019.	Carry's Confession.	
1032.	Caste.	
996.	Castle Avon,	Mrs. Marsh.

NO.	TITLE.	AUTHOR.
982.	Caxtons,	Edward Lytton Bulwer.
1052.	Cecil's Tryst,	James Payn.
967.	Chance Medley,	Thomas Colley Gratton.
998.	Charles Auchester,	E. Berger.
1034.	Charllotte's Inheritance,	M. E. Braddon.
960.	Chatsworth,	Ward.
973.	Chronicles of Clovernook,	Douglass Jerrold.
971.	Chevalier D'Harmental,	Alexander Dumas.
975.	Cinq-Mars,	Alfred De Vigny.
1032.	Circe,	Babington White.
970.	Citizen of Prague,	Mary Howitt.
1028.	Claverings,	Anthony Trollope.
1005.	Clerical Life,	George Eliot.
998.	Clouded Happiness,	Countess D'Orsay.
972.	Commander of Malta,	Eugene Sue.
989.	Commissioner,	G. P. R. James.
1002.	Constance Herbert,	Geraldine E. Jewsbury.
984.	Constance Lyndsay,	C. G. H.
978.	Convict,	G. P. R. James.
1015.	Cousin Phillis,	Mrs. Gaskell.
1011.	Countess Gisella,	E. Marlitt.
1001.	Country Neighborhood,	Miss E. A. Dupuy.
1027.	Cradock Nowell,	Richard Doddrige Blackmore.
1032.	Curate's Discipline,	Mrs. Eiloart.
1047.	Daisy Nichol,	Lady Hardy.
994.	Daltons,	Charles Lever.
1044.	Dangerous Guest.	
975.	Daniel Dennison.	Mrs. Hofland.
993.	Darien,	Eliot Warburton.
1011.	Dark Night's Work,	Mrs. Gaskell.
1050.	Daughter of Heth,	William Black.
990.	Daughter of Night,	S. W. Fullom.
1007.	Day's Ride,	Charles Lever.
1036.	Dead Sea Fruit,	M. E. Braddon.
1018.	Dennis Downe,	Annie Thomas.
1016.	Dennis Duval,	W. M. Thackeray.
966.	De Rohan,	Eugene Sue.
953.	Devereux,	Edward Lytton Bulwer.

NO.	TITLE.	AUTHOR.
981.	Discipline of Life.	
953.	Disowned,	Edward Lytton Bulwer.
998.	Dodd Family Abroad,	Charles Lever.
1056.	Dr. Wainright's Patient,	Edmund Yates.
1051.	Durnton Abbey,	Thomas Adolphus Trollope.
1047.	Earl's Dene,	R. E Francillon.
976.	Ehrenstein,	G. P. R. James.
1013.	Eleanora's Victory,	M. E. Braddon.
1955.	Ernest Maltravers,	Edward Lytton Bulwer.
1044.	Estelle Russell.	
954.	Eugene Aram,	Edward Lytton Bulwer.
1003.	Evelyn Marston,	Mrs. Marsh.
1052.	Fair to See,	L. W. M. Lockhart.
993.	Falkenburg.	
957.	False Heir,	G. P. R. James.
1039.	False Colors,	Annie Thomas.
974.	Father Darcy,	Mrs. Marsh.
1024.	Felix Holt,	George Eliot.
972.	Female Minister.	
1048.	Fenton's Quest,	M. E. Braddon.
1010.	First Friendship.	
1034.	Five Hundred Pounds Reward.	A Barrister.
992.	Florence Sackville,	Mrs. Burbury.
1050.	For Lack of Gold,	Charles Gibbon.
1056.	For the King,	Charles Gibbon.
956.	Forest Days,	G. P. R. James.
969.	Foster Brother,	Leigh Hunt.
975.	Fortescue,	James Sheridan Knowles.
1003.	Fortunes of Glencore,	Charles Lever.
1039.	Found Dead,	James Payn.
1046.	From Thistles—Grapes,	Eiloart.
965.	Gambler's Wife,	Mrs. Grey.
973.	Genevieve,	A. De Lamartine.
1006.	Gerald Fitzgerald,	Charles Lever.
1023.	Gilbert Rugge.	
1054.	Good Investment,	William Flagg.
1058.	Godolphin.	Edward Lytton Bulwer.
990.	Gold Worshipers.	

NO.	TITLE.	AUTHOR.
1054.	Golden Sorrow,	Mrs. Cashel Hoey.
980.	Gowrie,	G. P. R. James.
962.	Grandfather,	Miss Ellen Pickering.
982.	Great Hoggarty Diamond,	William M. Thackeray.
983.	Green Hand.	
1053.	Grif, Story of Australian Life,	B. L. Farjeon.
959.	Grumbler,	Miss Ellen Pickering.
1033½.	Guild Court,	George Macdonald.
1020.	Guy Deverell,	J. S. Le Fanu.
1043.	Gwendoline's Harvest,	James Payn.
1020.	Half a Million,	Amelia B. Edwards.
1020.	Hand-and-Glove,	Amelia B. Edwards.
985.	Hands, Not Hearts,	Janet W. Wilkinson.
1000.	Hard Times,	Charles Dickens.
980.	Harold,	Edward Lytton Bulwer.
1063.	Harry Heathcote,	Anthony Trollope.
993.	Head of the Family,	Miss Mulock.
1060.	He Cometh Not, She Said,	Annie Thomas.
974.	Heidelberg,	G. P. R. James.
1002.	Heiress of Haughton,	Mrs. Marsh.
1045.	Heir Expectant.	
995.	Henry Esmond,	William M. Thackeray.
989.	Henry Smeaton,	G. P. R. James.
960.	Heretic,	Lajétchnikoff.
1062.	Her Face Was Her Fortune,	F. W. Robinson.
1049.	Her Lord and Master,	Florence Marryatt.
1038.	Hetty,	Henry Kingsley.
962.	H——— Family,	Frederika Bremer.
1041.	Hirell,	John Saunders.
1055.	Hope Deferred,	Eliza F. Pollard.
1059.	Hour and the Man,	Harriet Martineau.
964.	Improvisatore,	Mary Howitt.
1045.	In Duty Bound.	
1060.	Innocent,	Mrs. Oliphant.
1038.	In Silk Attire,	William Black.
994.	Ivar,	Miss Carlen
959.	Jack of the Mill,	William Howitt.
979.	Jane Eyre,	Currer Bell.

NO.	TITLE.	AUTHOR.
1035.	Jeanie's Quiet Life.	
971.	Jessie's Flirtations.	
1043.	John,	Mrs. Oliphant.
1003.	John Halifax,	Miss Mulock.
1013.	John Marchmont,	M. E. Braddon.
1051.	Joshua Marvel.	
1062.	Joseph the Jew.	
987.	Julia Howard,	Mrs. Martin Bell.
1038.	Kathleen.	
996.	Katie Stewart,	Mrs. Oliphant.
1059.	Kenelon Chillingly,	Edward Lytton Bulwer.
1043.	Kilmeny,	William Black.
1025.	Kissing the Rod,	Edmund Yates.
1040.	Kitty,	M. Betham Edwards.
1015.	Ladder of Life,	Amelia B. Edwards.
991.	Lady and the Priest,	Mrs. Maberly.
998.	Lady Lee's Widowhood.	
969.	Lady of Milan,	Mrs. Thomson.
1024.	Land at Last,	Fdmund Yates.
954.	Last Days of Pompeii,	Edward Lytton Bulwer.
956.	Last of the Barons,	Edward Lytton Bulwer.
979.	Last of the Fairies,	G. P. R. James.
1058.	Leila,	Edward Lytton Bulwer.
1004.	Leonora D'Orco,	G. P. R. James.
974.	Leotine.	Mrs. Maberley.
973.	Lettice Arnold,	Mrs. Marsh.
963.	Libussa,	J. H. Musæus.
1006.	Life For a Life,	Miss Mulock.
995.	Life of Vicissitudes,	G. P. R James.
1049.	Life's Assize,	Mrs. H. Riddell.
1023.	Little Ragamuffin,	James Greenwood.
1012.	Live It Down,	J. C. Jeaffreson.
973.	Livonian Tales.	
1026.	Lizzie Lorton,	E. Lyman Linton.
964.	Look to the End,	Mrs. Ellis.
1036.	Lost Name,	J. S. Le Fanu.
957.	Lost Ship,	Captain Neale.
1063.	Lottie Darling,	J. C. Jeaffreson.

NO.	TITLE.	AUTHOR.
969.	Love and Mesmerism,	Horace Smith.
1036.	Love Or Marriage,	William Black.
1017.	Lovel the Widower,	W. M. Thackeray.
1051.	Lovels of Arden,	M. E. Braddon.
997.	Lover's Stratagem,	Emile Flygare Carlen.
974.	Lucretia,	Edward Lytton Bulwer.
988.	Luttrells,	Folkstone Williams.
1033.	Mabel's Progress.	
1027.	Madonna Mary,	Mrs. Oliphant.
964.	Maid of Honor.	
986.	Maid of Orleans.	
1055.	Maid of Sker,	R. D. Blackmore.
1016.	Margaret Denzil.	
1033½.	Margaret's Engagement.	
978.	Margaret Graham,	G. P. R. James.
976.	Marriage,	Miss S. Ferrier.
1012.	Martin Pole,	John Saunders.
977.	Martins of Chro' Martin,	Charles Lever.
981.	Mary Barton,	Mrs. Gaskell.
1012.	Mary Lindsay,	Emily Ponsonby.
1017.	Mattie A—— Stray.	
1053.	Maud Mohen,	Annie Thomas.
1016.	Maurice Dering,	George Lawrence.
992.	Maurice Tiernay,	Charles Lever.
1022.	Maxwell Drewitt,	F. G. Trafford.
1039.	Meta's Faith.	
982.	Midnight Sun,	Frederika Bremer.
978.	Midsummer Eve,	Mrs. S. C. Hall.
1037.	Mildred,	Georgianna M. Craik.
1007.	Mill On the Floss,	George Eliot.
1040.	Minister's Wife,	Mrs. Oliphant.
1006.	Misrepresentation,	Anna H Drury.
1019.	Miss Carew,	Amelia B. Edwards.
1018.	Miss Mackenzie,	Anthony Trollope.
1022.	Miss Majoribanks,	Mrs. Oliphant.
1009.	Mistress and Maid,	Miss Mulock.
1048.	Monarch of Mincing Lane,	William Black.
983.	Mordaunt Hall,	Mrs. Marsh.

NO.	TITLE.	AUTHOR.
1000.	Mother's Recompense,	Grace Aguilar.
1030.	Mr. Wynyard's Ward,	Holme Lee.
1059.	Murphy's Master,	James Payn.
1017.	My Brother's Wife,	Amalie B. Edwards.
1005.	My Lady Ludlow,	Mrs. Gaskell.
996.	My Novel,	Edward Lytton Bulwer.
983.	My Uncle the Curate.	
955.	Nabob at Home.	
1037.	Nature's Nobleman.	
985.	Ned Allen,	David Hannay.
957.	Neighbors,	Frederika Bremer.
1059.	New Magdalen,	Wilkie Collins.
986.	Night and Morning,	Edward Lytton Bulwer.
1031.	No Man's Friend,	Frederick William Robinson.
1030.	Nora and Archibald Lee.	
977.	Norman's Bridge,	Mrs. Marsh.
1001.	North and South,	Mrs. Gaskell.
1004.	Nothing New,	Miss Mulock.
1008.	Notice to Quit,	W. G. Wills.
1002.	Old Dominion,	G. P. R. James.
987.	Old Oak Chest,	G. P. R. James.
989.	Olive,	Miss Mulock.
1009.	Olive Blake's Good Work,	John Cordy Jeaffreson.
1055.	Ombra,	Mrs. Oliphant.
1018.	On Guard,	Annie Thomas.
1034.	One of the Family,	James Payn.
1007.	One of Them,	Charles Lever.
968.	Only a Fiddler,	Hans Christian Anderson.
1041.	Only Herself,	Annie Thomas.
968.	O. T.,	Hans Christian Anderson.
1056.	Passions in Letters,	Annie Thomas.
967.	Parsonage of Mora,	Frederika Bremer.
1052.	Patty,	Katharine S. Macquoid.
953.	Paul Clifford,	Edward Lytton Bulwer.
972.	Peers and Parvenus,	Mrs. Gore.
953.	Pelham,	Edward Lytton Bulwer.
988.	Petticoat Government,	Mrs. Trollope.
994.	Pequineillo,	G. P. R. James.

NO.	TITLE.	AUTHOR.
1024.	Phemie Keller,	F. G. Trafford.
956.	Pilgrims of the Rhine,	Edward Lytton Bulwer.
1029.	Played Out,	Annie Thomas.
1033½.	Playing for High Stakes,	Annie Thomas.
1011.	Point of Honor.	
1035.	Poor Humanity,	F. W. Robinson.
961.	Prairie Bird,	Charles Augustus Murray.
958.	President's Daughter,	Frederika Bremer.
987.	Pride.	
1062.	Princess of Thule,	William Black.
1009.	Professor's Lady,	Berthold Auerbach.
1063.	Publicans and Sinners,	Miss M. E. Braddon.
970.	Queen of Denmark,	Mrs. Gore.
999.	Quiet Heart,	Mrs. Oliphant.
1016.	Quite Alone,	George Augustus Sala.
1026.	Race for Wealth,	Mrs. J. H. Riddell.
1013.	Rachel Ray,	Anthony Trollope.
1028.	Rachel's Secret.	
1030.	Raymond's Heroine.	
992.	Ravenscliffe,	Mrs. Marsh.
963.	Regent's Daughter,	Charles H. Town.
987.	Reginald Hastings,	Eliot Warburton.
954.	Rienzi,	Edward Lytton Bulwer.
1058.	Robin Gray,	Charles Gibbon.
976.	Roland Cashel,	Charles Lever.
961.	Rose D'Albert,	G. P. R. James.
1004.	Rose of Ashurst,	Mrs. Marsh.
970.	Royal Favorite,	Mrs. Gore.
977.	Russell,	G. P. R. James.
964.	Safia,	Roger De Beauvoir.
1023.	Sans Merci,	George Lawrence.
966.	Self.	
979.	Self Control,	Mary Brunton.
955.	Self Devotion,	Miss Campbell.
984.	Shirley.	Currer Bell.
984.	Sidonia, the Sorceress,	William Meinhold.
1061.	Simpleton,	Charles Reade.
977.	Simple Story,	Mrs. Inchbald.

NO.	TITLE.	AUTHOR.
988.	Singleton Fontenoy,	James Hannay.
1027.	Sir Brook Fossbrooke,	Charles Lever.
985.	Sir Edward Graham,	Catherine Sinclair.
1047.	Sir Harry Hotspur,	Anthony Trollope.
999.	Sir Jasper Carew,	Charles Lever.
979.	Sir Theodore Broughton,	G. P. R. James.
1042.	So Runs the World Away,	Mrs. A. C. Steele.
1029.	Sowing the Wind,	E. Lynn Linton.
966.	Smuggler,	G. P. R. James.
1043.	Stern Necessity,	F. W. Robinson.
971.	Step Mother,	G. P. R. James.
1057.	Strange Adventures of a Pheaton,	William Black.
1008.	Strange Story,	Edward Lytton Bulwer.
1061.	Strangers and Pilgrims,	Miss M. E. Braddon.
990.	Stuart of Dunleath,	Caroline Norton.
1011.	St. Olaves.	
1006.	Sword and Gown,	George Lawrence.
1010.	Sylvia's Lovers,	Mrs. Gaskell.
963.	Tales from the German.	
1033.	Tenants of Malory,	J. S. Le Fanu.
1038.	That Boy of Norcotts,	Charles Lever.
1026.	The Beauclercs, Father and Son,	Charles Clarke.
1037.	The Bramleighs,	Charles Lever.
954.	The Czarina,	Mrs. Hofland.
1036.	The Dower House,	Annie Thomas.
970.	The Elves, etc.	Tieck.
991.	The Fate,	G. P. R. James.
982.	The Forgery,	G. P. R. James.
957.	The Home,	Frederika Bremer.
984.	The Ogilvies,	Miss Mulock.
960.	The Jew,	Spindler.
962.	The Jilt.	
1046.	The Warden,	Anthony Trollope.
985.	The Wilmingtons,	Mrs. Marsh.
1018.	Theodore Leigh,	Annie Thomas.
981.	Thirty Years Since,	G. P. R. James.
981.	Three Sisters, and Their Fortunes,	G. H. Lewes.
999.	Ticonderoga,	G. P. R. James.

NO.	TITLE.	AUTHOR.
989.	Time the Avenger,	Mrs. Marsh.
1022.	Toilers of the Sea,	Victor Hugo.
1057.	To the Bitter End,	M. E. Braddon.
1060.	Too Soon,	Katharine S. Macquoid.
961.	Triumphs of Time,	Mrs. Marsh.
1044.	True to Herself,	F. W. Robinson.
992.	Tutors Ward.	
1061.	Two Widows,	Annie Thomas.
1017.	Uncle Silas,	J. S. Le Fanu.
1041.	Under Foot,	Alton Clyde.
959.	Unloved One,	Mrs. Hofland.
965.	Veronica,	Zschokke.
1044.	Veronica.	
1028.	Village on the Cliff,	Miss Thackeray.
997.	Villette,	Currer Bell.
1045.	Vivian Romance,	Mortimer Collins.
1021.	Walter Goring,	Annie Thomas.
1033.	Waterdale Neighbors.	
978.	Way Side Cross,	E. H. Milman.
1015.	What Will He Do With It?	Edward Lytton Bulwer.
1045.	Which Is The Heroine?	
968.	White Boy,	Mrs. S. C. Hall.
967.	White Slave.	
1014.	Wife's Evidence,	W. G. Wills.
990.	Wife's Sister,	Mrs. Hubback.
976.	Woman's Trials,	Mrs. S. C. Hall.
1057.	Woman's Vengeance,	James Payn.
1049.	Won—Not Wood,	James Payn.
983.	Woodman,	G. P. R. James.
1039.	Wretched in Port,	Edmund Yates.
965.	Wyoming.	
1000.	Young Husband,	Mrs. Grey.
986.	Zanoni,	Edward Lytton Bulwer.
965.	Zoe,	Geraldine E. Jewsburry.
1063½.	Chronicles of Clovernook,	Douglass Jerold.
1063½.	Memories of my Youth,	Alphonso de Lamertine.

Whole Number 406.

PUBLIC DOCUMENTS.

NO.	TITLE.	STATE.
268.	Acts and Resolutions of the United	States, 1867—1868.
269.	" "	" 1869—1870.
453.	" "	" 1873—1874.
395.	Acts and Resoluions of Massachusetts, 1869.	
337.	Adjutant General's Report,	Arkansas, 1861–1866.
404.	Adjutant General's Report,	Connecticut, 1861–1864.
338–45.	Adjutant General's Report, Vol. 1–8,	Illinois, 1861–1866.
346–53.	Adjutant General's Report, Vol. 1–8,	Indiana, 1861–1865.
354–5.	Adjutant General's and Quartermaster's Report, Vol. 1, 2,	Iowa, 1863.
356.	Adjutant General and Quartermaster's Report,	Iowa, 1864.
357.	Adjutant General and Quartermaster's Report,	Iowa, 1864–1865.
358.	Adjutant General and Quartermaster's Report,	Iowa, 1865–1866.
359–60.	Adjutant General and Quartermaster's Report, Vol. 1, 2,	Iowa, 1867.
458.	Adjutant General's Report,	Iowa, 1868.
459.	" " "	" 1873.
460.	" " "	" 1874.
416.	Adjutant General and Quartermaster's Report, Vol. 1,	Kansas, 1861–1865.
417.	Adjutant General and Quartermaster's Report,	Kansas, 1864.
1–2.	Adjutant General's Report, Vol. 1, 2,	Kentucky, 1861–1866.
361.	Adjutant General's Report,	Maine, 1861.
362.	" " "	" 1862.

NO.	TITLE.	STATE.
363.	Adjutant General's Report,	Maine, 1863.
364.	" " " Volume 1,	" 1864–1865.
365.	" " " Appendix D,	" 1864–1865.
366.	" " "	" 1866.
2. (1, 2)	Adjut't Gen's Report, Vol. 42,	Massachusetts, 1861–1865.
367.	" " "	" 1863.
367. (1)	" " "	" 1864.
367. (2)	" " "	" 1868.
368.	Adjutant General's Report,	Michigan, 1862.
369.	" " "	" 1863.
370.	" " "	" 1864.
371–3.	" " " Vol. 1, 2, 3,	" 1865–1866.
440.	" " "	" 1874.
374.	Adjutant General's Report,	Minnesota, 1861–1866.
375.	Adjutant General's Report,	Missouri, 1865.
376–7.	Adjutant General's Report, Vol. 1, 2,	New Hampshire, 1865.
378–9.	" " " " 1, 2,	" 1866.
380.	" " "	" 1868.
381.	Adjutant General's Report,	New York, 1867.
382–4.	" " " Vol. 1, 2, 3,	" 1868.
392.	Adjutant General's Report,	Pennsylvania, 1866.
393.	Adjutant General's Report,	Rhode Island, 1861–1865.
$395\frac{1}{2}$.	Adjutant and Inspector Gen's Report,	Vermont, 1862.
396.	" " " "	" 1864.
397.	" " " "	" 1864–1865.
398.	" " " "	" 1865–1866.
399.	Adjutant General's Report,	West Virginia, 1864.
400.	" " "	" 1865.
401.	Adjutant General's Report,	Wisconsin, 1864.
402.	" " "	" 1864.
403.	" " "	" 1865.
$403\frac{1}{2}$.	Adj't and Quartermaster Gen's Report,	" 1867.
313.	Agricultural Report,	Massachusetts, 1861.
314,	" "	" 1863.
315.	" "	" 1866–1867.
316,	" "	" 1867–1868.
317.	" "	" 1868–1869.
302.	Agricultural Report,	United States, 1864–1865.

NO.	TITLE.	STATE.	
303.	Agricultural Report,	United States,	1865–1866.
304.	" "	"	1866.
305.	" "	"	1866–1867.
306.	" "	"	1867.
307.	" "	"	1867–1868.
308.	" "	"	1868.
309.	" "	"	1868–1869.
310.	" "	"	1869.
311.	" "	"	1870.
312.	" "	"	1871.
446.	" "	"	1873.
318.	" "	Wisconsin,	1861–1868.
318½.	" "	"	1871.
418.	Army of the Potomac,		1861–1862.
427.	Army Register,		1863.
428.	" "		1864.
429.	" "		1865.
430.	" "		1866.
431,	" "		1867.
432.	" "	(January)	1868.
433.	" "	(August)	1868.
434.	" "	(January)	1869.
435.	" "	(September)	1869.
436.	" "		1870.
437.	" "	(January)	1871.
442.	" "		1875.
461.	Army Re-union, Chicago,		1868.
462.	Army of the Cumberland Re-union,		1868.
463.	" " "		1869.
464.	" " "		1870.
465.	" " "		1871.
466.	" " "		1872.
467.	" " "		1873.
468.	" " "		1874.
266.	Census Report,	Abstract,	1852.
265.	" "	Preliminary,	1860.
18.	" "	Population,	1860.
19,	" "	Manufactures,	1860.

NO.	TITLE.		YEAR.
20.	Census Report,	Mortality, etc.,	1860.
21.	" "	Agriculture,	1860.
22.	" "	Population, etc.,	1870.
267.	" "	Compendium	1870.
23.	" "	Industry and Wealth,	1870.
238–9.	Claims, Court of, Vol. 1, 2,		1861–1862.
240.	" "		1862–1863.
241.	Claims Against China,		1868–1869.
24.	Coast Survey, Report,		1863.
25.	" " "		1864–1865.
26.	" " "		1865–1866.
27.	" " "		1866–1867.
28.	" " "		1867–1868.
193½.	Commerce and Navigation,		1851.
194.	Commerce and Navigation, Report,		1862–1863.
195.	" " "		1863.
196.	" " "		1864–1865.
197.	" " "		1865–1866.
198.	" " "		1866–1867.
199.	" " "		1867–1868.
200.	" " "		1868–1869.
201.	" " "		1871.
202.	Commercial Relations, Report, Vol. 10,		1863–1864.
203.	" " "		1864–1865.
204.	" " "		1865–1866.
205.	" " "		1866–1867.
206.	" " "		1867–1868.
207.	" " "		1868–1869.
226.	Conduct of War, Report, Part 1,		1863.
226½.	" " " " 2,		1863.
226½.	" " " " 3,		1863.
227.	" " "		1864.
228-30.	" " "	Part 1, 2, 3,	1864–1865.
231-3.	" " "	Vol. 1, 2, 3,	1865.
234-5	" " "	Supplement, Vol. 1, 2,	1865–1866.
236-7.	" " "	" Part 1, 2,	1866.
456.	Congressional Directory,		1875.

NO.	TITLE.	YEAR.
3-4.	Congressional Globe, Part 1, 2,	1860–1861.
5-7.	" " " 1, 2, 3,	1868–1869.
8.	" " Appendix,	1869.
9.	" " Part 1,	1871.
10.	" " Part 2 and Appendix,	1871.
11-15.	" " Part 1, 2, 3, 4, 5,	1871–1872.
16.	" " Appendix,	1871–1872.
17.	" " Index,	1871–1872.
36. (1)	Congressional Record, Vol. 1, 43d Congress, Special Session, Senate,	1873.
36. (2)	Congressional Record, Index to Vol. 2, Parts 1-6, First Session, 43d Congress,	1874.
36. (3-8)	Congressional Record, Vol. 2, Parts 1-6, First Session, 43d Congress,	1874.
37.	Congressional Report,	1842.
255.	Contested Elections,	1864–1865.
391.	Corporation Ordinance,	1859.
96-9.	Diplomatic Correspondence, Part 1, 2, 3, 4,	1864–1865.
100-3.	" " Part 1, 2, 3, 4,	1865–1866.
104-6.	" " Vol. 1, 2, 3,	1866–1867.
107-8.	" " " 1, 2,	1867–1868.
109.	" " " 1,	1868–1869.
110.	" " " 2,	1868–1869.
264.	Education, Report,	1871.
260.	Estimates of Appropriations,	1864–1865.
33.	Executive Documents, Vol. 15, Part 1,	1853–1854.
38.	" "	1861.
39-41.	" " Vol. 1, 2, 3,	1861–1862.
35.	" " " 4,	" "
42.	" " " 5,	" "
43-44.	" " " 5, Part 2, 3,	" "
34.	" " " 6,	" "
45-50.	" " " 7-12,	" "
51-5.	" " " 1-5,	1862–1863.
56.	" " " 5, Maps,	" "
57-9.	" " " 6, 7, 8,	" "
36.	" " " 9,	" "
60-1.	" " " 10, Part 1, 2,	" "

NO.	TITLE.	YEAR.
62-3.	Executive Documents, Vol. 11, 12,	1862–1863.
64-6.	" " " 1, 2, 3,	1863–1864.
67.	" " " 4,	" "
68-9.	" " " 6, 7,	" "
70.	" " " 9,	" "
71.	" " " 13,	" "
72-3.	" " " 15, 16,	" "
74.	" " Maps,	" "
75-6.	" "	1864–1865.
77-81.	" "	1865–1866.
82-8.	" "	1866–1867.
89.	" "	1867.
89. (1)	" "	1867–1868.
89. (2)	" "	" "
90.	" "	" "
90. (1)	" "	" "
90. (2)	" "	" "
90. (3)	" "	" "
90. (4)	" "	" "
91.	" "	" "
91. (1)	" "	" "
91. (2)	" "	" "
92-4.	" "	1868–1869.
94. (1)	" "	" "
95.	" "	" "
32.	Explorations, Nevada and Arizona,	1871.
259.	Finance Report,	1853–1854.
454.	" "	1874.
227.	Fort Pillow Massacre,	1864.
405.	General Orders, Volunteer Force,	1861–1863.
406.	" " War Department,	1862.
407.	" " Index,	"
408.	" " War Department, No. 1-239,	1863.
409.	" " " " 240-400,	"
410.	" " Index,	"
411.	" " War Department,	1864.
412.	" " Veteran Reserve Corps,	"

NO.	TITLE.	YEAR.
413.	General Orders, Courts Martial, No. 1-165,	1864.
414.	" " " " " 166-409,	"
415.	" " War Department,	1865.
273.	General Pope's Virginia Campaign, Report,	1863.
111-14.	House Committee's Report, Vol. 1, 2, 3, 4,	1861–1862.
115.	" " Vol. 1,	1863–1864.
116.	" "	1864–1865.
117-19.	" " Vol. 1, 2, 3,	1865–1866.
120-3.	" "	1866–1867.
124.	" "	1867.
125.	" "	1867–1868.
126.	" "	" "
127.	" "	1868–1869.
128.	" " Vol. 2,	" "
129.	House Journal,	1862–1863.
130.	" "	1863–1864.
131.	" "	1864–1865.
132.	" "	1865–1866.
133.	" "	1866–1867.
134.	" "	1867.
135.	" "	1867–1868,
136.	" "	1868–1869.
137.	House, Miscellaneous,	1861.
138.	" "	1861–1862.
139-40.	" " Vol. 1, 2,	1862–1863.
141-3.	" " " 1, 2, 3,	1863–1864.
144.	" "	1864–1865.
145.	" "	1865–1866.
146.	" "	" "
147.	" "	" "
148.	" "	1866–1867.
149-50.	" " Vol. 1, 2,	1867.
151-2.	" " " 1, 2,	1867–1868.
153.	" "	1868–1869.
271.	Immigration Report,	1871–1872.
457.	" "	1873.
270.	Indian Commissioners' Report,	1871.
385.	Inspector General's Report, New York,	1867.

NO.	TITLE.	YEAR.
386.	Justices' Report, New York,	1831.
330.	Ku-Klux Conspiracy, Report, Vol. 2, North Carolina,	1872.
331-3.	Ku-Klux Conspiracy, Report, Vol. 3, 4, 5, South Carolina,	1872.
334-5.	Ku-Klux Conspiracy, Report, Vol. 11, 12, Mississippi,	1872.
336.	Ku-Klux Conspiracy, Report, Vol. 13, Florida and Mississippi,	1872.
263.	Land Office, Report,	1867.
388.	Laws of New York,	1839.
389.	Legislative Documents, New York,	1839.
390.	" " "	1841.
319.	Message and Documents,	1840.
320-1.	" " Parts 1, 2,	1853–1854.
322.	" "	1860.
323-6.	" " Parts 1, 2, 3, 4,	1862–1863.
327.	" " Abridgement,	1868–1869.
328.	" " Part 1,	1871–1872.
329.	" " (Departm't of State)	" "
444.	" " Abridgment,	1873–1874.
447-8.	" " Parts 1, 2, (Interior)	" "
449.	" " (State)	1874–1875.
450.	" " (Navy, P. M. Gen.—Attorney General)	1874–1875.
251-2.	Mexican Affairs, Parts 1, 2,	1865–1866.
253.	" "	1866–1867.
29.	Military Commission to Europe—Major R. Delafield,	1854–1856.
30.	Military Commission to Europe—Captain G. B. McClellan,	1855–1856.
31.	Military Commission to Europe—Major A. Mordicai,	1855–1856.
254.	Mineral Resources of the United States, Report,	1867–1868.
272.	Mortality on Emigrant Ships,	1854.
425.	National Almanac and Record,	1863.
426.	" " "	1864.
443.	National War Manual,	1862.

NO.	TITLE.	YEAR.
219. (1)	Navy and Marine Corps, Register,	1864.
256,	Ordnance Stores, Report,	1863.
257.	Ordnance, Contracts,	1867–1868.
274.	Patent Office Report, Mechanics, Part 1,	1853.
275-7.	" " " " Vol. 1, 2, 3,	1856.
278-9.	" " " " " 1, 2,	1863.
280-1.	" " " " Part 1, 2,	1864–1865.
282-4.	" " " " Vol. 1, 2, 3,	1865–1866.
285-6.	" " " " " 1, 2,	1866.
287-9.	" " " " " 1, 2, 3,	1866–1867.
290-3.	" " " " " 1, 2, 3, 4,	1867.
294-7.	" " " " " 1, 2, 3, 4,	1867–1868.
298-301.	" " " " " 1, 2, 3, 4,	1867–1868.
438.	Political Manual,	1866–1867.
439.	Prevention and Repression of Crime— (International Congress)	1872.
258.	Prize Cases in New York, Vol 14,	1863–1864.
469.	Railroad Returns (Massachusetts)	1868.
	Roll of Honor (Giving Name, Company and Regiment of Union Soldiers Interred in National Cemeteries.)	
469.	Roll of Honor, Vol. 1-4 and No. 1- 7.	
470.	" " " 8-11.	
471.	" " " 12-15.	
472.	" " " 16-17.	
473.	" " " 18-20.	
474.	" " " 21-23.	
475.	" " " 24-27.	
242.	Secretary of Interior and Postmaster General's Report,	1864–1865.
243.	Secretary of Interior Report,	1865–1866.
244.	" " "	1866–1867.
245.	" " "	1867–1868.
246.	" " "	1868–1869.
220.	Secretary of Navy Report,	1864–1865.
221.	" " "	1865–1866.
222.	Secretary of Navy and Postmaster Gen's Report,	1866–1867.

NO.	TITLE.	YEAR.
223.	Secretary of Navy and Postmaster Gen's Report,	1867–1868.
224.	" " " " "	1868–1869.
225.	Secretary of Navy Report,	1872.
208.	Secretary of War and General-in-Chief's Report,	1863.
209.	Secretary of War and Postmaster Gen's Report, Vol. 5,	1863–1864.
210.	Secretary of War Report,	1864–1865.
211.	" " " Part 1,	1865–1866.
212.	" " " Appendix 1,	" "
213.	" " " Part 2,	" "
214.	" " " Appendix to Part 2,	" "
215.	" " "	1866–1867.
216-17.	" " " Vol. 1, 2,	1867–1868.
218-19.	" " " " 1, 2,	1868–1869.
154.	Senate Documents, Vol. 1,	1845.
155.	" "	1861.
156-61.	" " Vol. 1, 2, 3, 4, 5, 6,	1861–1862.
162.	" " Maps,	" "
163.	" "	1862–1863.
164.	" "	1863,
165.	" "	1863–1864.
166.	" "	1864–1865.
167.	" "	1865–1866.
168.	" "	" "
169-70.	" " Vol. 1, 2,	1866–1867,
171.	" "	1867.
172.	Senate Journal,	1861.
173.	" "	1861–1862.
174.	" "	1862–1863.
175.	" "	1863–1864.
176.	" "	1865–1866.
177.	" "	1866–1867.
178.	" "	1867.
179.	Senate, Miscellaneous,	1861–1862.
180.	" "	1862–1863.
181.	" "	1863–1864.
182.	" "	1865–1866.
183.	" "	1866–1867.

NO.	TITLE.	YEAR.
184.	Senate Reports,	1861–1862.
185-8.	" " Vol. 1, 2, 3, 4,	1862–1863.
189.	" "	1863–1864.
190.	" "	1864–1865.
191.	" "	1865–1866.
192.	" "	1866–1867.
193.	" "	1867.
247.	Smithsonian Report,	1863–1864.
248.	" "	1864–1865.
249.	" "	1865–1866.
250.	" "	1868–1869.
455.	Sumner, Charles, Memorial Addresses, April 27,	1874.
387.	Statute Manual, New York,	1831.
451-2.	Transportation Routes to Seabard, Vol. 1, 2,	1874.
261.	Trial of Henry Wirz,	1867–1868.
262.	Troubles in Kansas,	1856.
394.	Wisconsin Statutes, Revised,	1858.
420.	Wisconsin Digest of Laws, E. A. Spencer,	1868.
421.	Wisconsin Legislative Manual,	1865.
422.	" " "	1871.
423.	" " "	1872.
424.	" " "	1874.
476.	" " "	1875.

482.	Herbaceous Plants and Quadrupeds of Mass., Chester Dewy,	1840.
481.	Memorial of Frederick Lyman Tremain, Late Lieut. Col. 10th N. Y. Cavalry,	1865.
480.	Navy Register,	1873.
441.	Report of National Home for D. V. S., Milwaukee,	1874.
477.	Secretary of Navy Report,	1869.
478.	" " "	1870.
479.	" " "	1871.
445.	United States Army Regulations (Revised),	1861.
483.	United States Postal Guide (January),	1875.

HOSPITAL LIBRARY

AT THE

NATIONAL HOME FOR DISABLED VOLUNTEER SOLDIERS,

NORTHWESTERN BRANCH,

Near Milwaukee, Wis.

JULY, 1875.

HOSPITAL LIBRARY.

NO.	TITLE.
3.	Appleton's Journal.
15.	Anatomy, Grey's.
36–43.	Agricultural Reports, 8V.
51–2.	Agricultural Reports, Wisconsin, 2 Vols.
47–8.	Adjutant General's Report, Wisconsin.
59–62.	Adjutant General's Report, Michigan.
75.	Adjutant General's Report, Minnesota.
58.	Adventures of Gil Blas.
121.	American Literature, Compendium.
78.	Atlantic Monthly.
132.	Autobiography of a Married Woman.
151–2.	Arctic Adventures.
207.	Arithmetic, Natural Introductory.
330.	Arithmetic, Practical.
343.	Alarm to Unconverted Sinners.
209.	Astronomy, Primary.
204.	Astronomy, 14 Weeks in.
210.	Arizona and Sonora.
228.	Art of War.
317.	American Angler.
318.	Acupuncturation, Treatise on.
325.	Agents' Manual.
333.	Artillery Hand-book.
30.	Administration of Buchanan.
46.	Acts and Resolves, 40th Congress.

NO.	TITLE.
243.	At Last.
102.	Bailey's Poetical Works.
106.	Bürger's Poems.
242.	Black Dwarf.
147.	Bleak House.
161–2.	Barnes' Notes.
248–9.	Bryant's Poems.
339.	Both Sides of the Sea.
322.	By-Gone Days In Our Village.
226.	Bressant.
32.	British Essayists, Modern.
313.	Barriers Burned Away.
33.	Bible.
154–6.	Channing's Works.
35.	Census, 9th, Compendium of, 1870.
108.	Chemistry, Town's.
131.	Crayon Sketches.
133.	Cometh Up As A Flower.
139.	Campaign of 1862—'63.
114.	Correlation of Forces.
141.	Charles Lever.
202.	Chess Book.
247.	Charles Lamb.
302.	Crust of the Cake.
157.	Devereaux.
24.	Dictionary, Musical.
239.	Dictionary of Antiquities.
19-20.	Daniel Webster, Life of.
21.	Dispensatory, American.
63.	Domestic Physician, Homeopathic.
211.	Deus Semper.
220.	Divine Character Vindicated.

NO.	TITLE.
301.	David Loyd's Last Will.
337.	Draytons and the Davinants.
1-2.	Encyclopedia, Zell's.
17	Encyclopedia of Wit and Humor.
65.	English Literature of the Nineteenth Century.
149.	Early Dawn.
252.	Ethelyn's Mistake.
327.	Early Crowned.
107.	Fruit Garden.
122.	Father Tom and the Pope.
140.	Fudge Doings.
129.	Forms of Water.
144.	Flora's Lexicon.
215.	Farm-book, American.
307.	Florence Rewarded.
310.	Florence Baldwin's Pic-nic.
319.	Foot-prints of Roger Williams.
335-8.	Family Library.
77.	Foreign Miscellany.
142.	German, Key to Short Course.
143	Geology, Fourteen Weeks In.
148.	Good-bye Sweet Heart.
201.	Grammar, Kerl's English.
202-3.	Grammar, English.
250.	Grandmother's Scrap-book
313.	Gustavus Adolphus.
68-70.	Harper's Magazine.
25-6.	History of France.
29.	History of Rome.
56.	History of the United States.
57.	History of Wisconsin.
27-8.	History of Civilization in England.
158.	History by Barbara.
159.	Heir of Redcliffe.
53.	House Journal of Dacotah
222.	Home as Found.
326.	Heman's Poems.
314.	Holidays at Roselands.
332.	Hale's United States.
72.	India, Lectures on.

NO.	TITLE.
223.	Ivanhoe.
342.	Infidelity, Reply to.
233.	If, Yes, and Perhaps.
232.	Ingham Papers.
164.	Journey Round the World.
334.	Judah's Lion.
336.	James' Traveler's Companion.
113.	Knick Knacks.
248.	King Authur.
55.	Law Register.
116.	Light and Electricity.
76.	Lippincott's Magazine.
117.	Lamps, Pitchers and Trumpets.
127-8.	Lives of Eminent Men.
339.	Letters to a Sister.
214.	Letters to the Joneses.
219.	Lessons in Life.
227.	Little Hodge.
235.	Livingstones of Livingstone.
244.	Laicus, by Lyman Abbott.
308,	Linvel's Courage.
324.	Land of the Forum and Vatican.
341.	Letters to Young Ladies.
10-14.	Meyer's Universal Magazine.
18.	Mrs. Gurney's Apology.
105.	Memoirs of Rev. Sidney Smith.
340.	Memoirs of Rev. J. B. Taylor.
145.	Margaret.
218.	Mother at Home.
163.	Mother's Recompense.
306.	Mother's Request.
231.	Maize or Indian Corn.
312.	Ministering Children.
316.	Madame Recamier.
323.	Margaret Warner.
253.	My Southern Friends.
331.	Map of New England.
315,	Materialization of the present Day.
124.	Notes of a Volunteer.
320.	Nothing To Say.

NO.	TITLE.
71.	North American Review.
115.	Neuralgia, Treatise on.
135.	Orchard Guide.
134.	Orpheus C. Kerr Papers.
240.	Ordeal for Wives.
300.	Occupation of a Retired Life.
238.	Ocean World.
31.	Philosophy, Dalton's.
112,	Philosophy of Herbert Spencer.
205.	Philosophy, Fourteen Weeks in.
208.	Philosophy, Natural.
225.	Philosophy, Home and Social.
234.	Philosophy, Proverbial.
236.	Philosophy, Upham's Mental.
329.	Physics.
243.	Physiology and Health.
246.	Papers for Home Reading.
229.	Poems, Mount Vernon.
130.	Poems, Huntington.
160.	Prison Life.
221.	Pastor of the Desert.
341.	Preciousness of Christ.
138.	Power of Religion.
120.	Peter Simple.
125.	Parent's Assistant.
109.	Psychology and Anthropology.
103.	Pentateuch.
34.	Patent Office Report.
44.	Report, State Board of Health, Mass.
49.	Report, 7th Annual, State Charities, Mass.
74.	Report, Board of Education, Mass.
50.	Report, Bureau of Statistics and Navigation, U. S., 1871.
64.	Reading and Oratory, Elements of.
101.	Rule or Ruin.
200.	Reader, 5th National.
206	Reader, 4th Independent.
217.	Roman Republic of 1849.
241.	Reptiles and Birds.
321.	Rolla and Luby.
66-7.	Surgeon Gen. Reports, U. S., 4, 5, 6, 7, 8, 9.
22-3.	Surgery, Gross.
104.	South Africa.
110.	Sound, by Tyndall.
111.	Social Statistics.
118.	Scripture Manual.
126.	Second War with England.
136-7.	Sermons by Dr. Spencer.
146.	Songs for Social and Public Worship.
224.	Sylvia's World.
309.	Stephen and His Tempter.
338.	Sunny Side Series.
340.	Stories of England.
150.	Temperance, Jewett.
303.	Tracts.
251.	The World As It Is.
304.	Text-book of Science.
305.	Thoughts on Personal Religion.
237.	Vegetable World.
119.	Wife's Stratagem.
123.	Watch-words for the Warfare of Life.
153,	Washington and His Generals.
216.	Wet Days at Edgewood.
230.	Where Is The City?
311.	Young Shetlander.
73.	Yucatan, by Stephens.

NOTE. Some of the books composing the Hospital Library were purchased by the Home, others were duplicates from the main library, but the greater part were obtained from publishers by solicitation of Dr. I. H. Stearns, Surgeon.

This library is placed in the Surgeon's Office and is under the Surgeon's care.

ERRATA.

Page 7,	Arabian Nights Entertainment,	should be No.		364.
" 9,	Baptism, Mode and Subject,......	"	"	2,217.
" 26,	Grif: Story of Australian Life,....	"	"	1,053.
" 43,	Luther, Martin, Life and Times of,	"	"	2,195.
" 44,	Marie Antoinette and Her Son,....	"	"	1,279.
" 44,	Marriage,........	"	"	976.
" 46,	Misrepresentation,................	"	"	1,006.
" 57,	Foul Play,...............	"	"	1,263.

GENERAL SUMMARY.

I. Library proper :

Highest Number on Volumes, ... 2,261,
* Fractional Numbers, etc., ... 12,

Number of Volumes .... 2,273.

Harper's Select Novels, 406 works bound in 113 Volumes. 406 less 113, ... 293,

Number of Works, ... 2,566.

II. Public Documents :

Highest Nnmber on Volumes, ... 483,
Fractional Numbers, etc., ... 28,

Number of Volumes, ... 511.

III. Hospital Library, ... 237.

Number of Volumes accounted for, ... 3,021.

Number of Volumes and Works accounted for, ... 3,314.

---

* When a book came to hand after the Library was numbered, fractional numbers, etc., were made use of to insert the book in its class.

NOTE. Number of *Volumes*, instead of Number of Works, to be given in the monthly reports.